I0709654

ISBN 978-90-04-69430-9

Full text of the General Course published in September 2023 in the *Recueil des cours*, Vol. 433.

Cover photograph: *Lady at the Virginals with a Gentleman,* by Johannes Vermeer.

THE HAGUE ACADEMY OF INTERNATIONAL LAW

*A collection of law lectures
in pocketbook form*

BRILL | NIJHOFF

2024

Parallel Proceedings
in International Arbitration

Theoretical Analysis and the Search
for Practical Solutions

Parallel Proceedings in International Arbitration

Theoretical Analysis and the Search for Practical Solutions

SALIM MOOLLAN

TABLE OF CONTENTS

INTRODUCTION

The issue of parallel proceedings is a long-standing and classical problem of international arbitration. The last major academic analysis of the issue in 2006 by the International Law Association and by the Geneva Colloquium on Consolidation of Proceedings in Investment Arbitration, led by Professor Kaufmann-Kohler. Since then, the development of investment arbitration in particular has exacerboted the problems faced in day-to-day practice, which these seminal studies have unfortunately only had limited impact in alleviating. With this in mind, now is an opportune moment to re-examine the issue through a fresh theoretical lens and renewed focus on finding practical solutions.

CHAPTER I

DEFINING THE SUBJECT: WHAT ARE PARALLEL PROCEEDINGS IN INTERNATIONAL ARBITRATION?

There is no official or formal definition of "parallel proceedings" in the context of international arbitration. The term has not been expressly defined in any legal instrument, treaty or statute. Rather, it is a term that has been introduced and developed through academic works, commentaries, books, essays, law review articles and blogs. As a result, defining the concept of parallel proceedings can be a challenging task.

However, despite the lack of a formal definition, it is crucial to make every effort to define the scope of the subject matter addressed in this course. This is not simply an academic pursuit. As Socrates noted centuries ago, definitions enable us to distil the essence of a concept, allowing us to think clearly and consistently. In other words, defining parallel proceedings is a prerequisite to conducting any meaningful analysis and discussion of our topic.

A. Defining parallel proceedings

1. "Connection" between different proceedings

While international arbitration lacks a formal definition of parallel proceedings, soft law instruments and under EU law provide definitions that can serve as a starting point for a modernised working definition. To begin with, it should be noted that different terms are used to refer to this phenomenon, including "concurrent", "multiple" and "multi-party" proceedings in English and *pendantes, concurrentes, multiples* or *connexes* proceedings in French. The French term *connexes* is particularly interesting because it does not have a direct equivalent in the English-language arbitral literature. It can be translated as "related", "interrelated" or "connected" proceedings.

It is crucial to recognise that each term does not necessarily capture the same phenomenon, and there are genuine differences of meaning that need to be bridged or explained. These terms can be rationalised into three distinct groups.

First, the terms "parallel" *(pendants)* or "concurrent" *(concurrentes)* proceedings focus on the time element, emphasising that the proceedings are progressing simultaneously or overlapping in time. These terms are inspired by and probably derive from the notion of *lis pendens*, but they do not fully cover the complexity and array of scenarios that fall under parallel proceedings. Connected proceedings running concurrently are just one *type* of parallel proceedings.

Second, the terms "multiple" *(multiples)* and "multiparty" *(multi-partite)* proceedings highlight the multiplicity of proceedings or parties, without reference to a time element or simultaneity. In one sense, the term "multiple proceedings" is not inaccurate: there must be more than one proceeding, a single proceeding cannot give rise to parallel proceedings, and thus, the existence of more than one proceeding is a prerequisite for parallel proceedings. But the term does not explain what these proceedings must have in common to be grouped under the same umbrella. While the terms "parallel" and "concurrent" are too narrow, "multiple" is too broad. The term "multiparty" also lends itself to confusion because parallel proceedings can occur between the same two parties, even if multiparty proceedings *can* give rise to parallel proceedings (e.g. in the context of interrelated contracts in commercial arbitrations).

Lastly, the terms "related", "interrelated" or "connected" proceedings are more accurate in capturing the subject matter of parallel proceedings. The French term *connexes* does not require simultaneity or a time element and is rightly broader than the terms "parallel" or "concurrent". It is also not as broad as "multiple" or "multiparty" proceedings. The term *connexes* and its English translations thus focus on the *two* core attributes of the definition of parallel proceedings: the existence of multiple *related* or *connected* proceedings.

2. Nature of the "connection"

Understanding the nature of the "connection" between multiple proceedings is crucial in grasping the definition of parallel proceedings. What *kind* of connection is required between multiple proceedings for them to qualify as parallel proceedings?

The International Law Association

The International Law Association ("ILA") provides a useful starting point with its definition proposed in the ILA "Recommendations on *Lis Pendens* and *Res Judicata* and Arbitration" in 2006:

> "[Parallel proceedings are] proceedings pending before a national court or another arbitral tribunal in which the parties and one or more of the issues are the same or substantially the same as the ones before the arbitral tribunal in the Current Arbitration."[1]

---

[1] F. De Ly and A. Sheppard, "ILA Recommendations on *Lis Pendens* and *Res Judicata* and Arbitration, Seventy-Second International Law Association Conference on International Commercial Arbitration, Toronto, Canada, 4-8 June 2006", *Arbitration International*, Vol. 25, No. 1 (2009), pp. 83-86 at p. 83.

This definition is now fifteen years old, and the field has developed since the ILA crafted it, particularly in investment treaty arbitration. For instance, the scenario of multiple claims by unrelated investors against the same State over the same measure was not then considered as a problem of parallel proceedings. Similarly, multiple claims again the same State by shareholders in the same corporate chain were a rare occurrence and would not have been at the forefront of ILA drafters' minds in 2006. The problem they had in mind would have been a more familiar one in the context of international arbitration: *lis pendens*, that is to say, connected proceedings running concurrently. But there are other limitations to this definition.

First, the definition includes a time element, requiring proceedings to be "pending". This aspect is too narrow as proceedings could still qualify as parallel, even if they are successive rather than concurrent, as long as they are connected in a meaningful way.

Second, the definition requires "the parties" to be "the same or substantially the same", which is not always the case in investment arbitration. For example, there may be parallel proceedings even if only one party is the same, such as in cases where several unrelated investors bring claims against the same State over the same measure. Similarly, in cases involving so-called "vertical claims" brought by shareholders from the same corporate chain, the parties need not be "the same or substantially the same". The same applies to a State enacting a measure affecting a pool of investors facing numerous claims over the "same or substantially the same issue", even if there are different claimants. These cases are "connected" by a common factual predicate – the same State measure.

Third, the definition requires "one or more of the issues" to be "the same or substantially the same". This requirement is correct for *factual* issues: for the proceedings to be related, there must be a common factual predicate. There must be one or more facts that are common to the parallel proceedings. However, to the extent it refers to *legal* issues, this is not necessarily the case. Legal issues can differ between proceedings due to varying applicable laws, including different bilateral investment treaties ("BITs"). Even if the same provision applies, such as the fair and equitable treatment ("FET") standard, there could still be differences in wording and substance, with FET being tied to the customary international law standard of minimum treatment of aliens in one case but not another.

On the first two points – proceedings being pending and between the same parties – the ILA definition appears to be too narrow. On the third point, it is too broad, for it fails to make a distinction between factual and legal issues.

The Brussels I Regulation (recast)

While it does not apply to international arbitration[2], the European Union's adoption of the Brussels I Regulation (recast) in 2012, which came into effect in 2015[3], provides an indirect definition of parallel proceedings in the context of international court litigation. The Regulation does not strictly define parallel proceedings, but Section 9, titled "*Lis pendens* – related actions", focuses on scenarios in which courts of Member States may stay proceedings, establishing a first-in-time rule where the court first seized of a cause of action within a Member State has jurisdiction over the dispute, and subsequent

---

[2] See Article 1 (2) *(d)* of the Brussels I Regulation (recast).

[3] Regulation (EU) No. 1215/2012 of the European Parliament and of the Council of 12 December 2012 on jurisdiction and the recognition and enforcement of judgments in civil and commercial matters (recast), https://eur-lex.europa.eu/LexUriServ/LexUriServ.do?uri=OJ:L:2012:351:0001:0032:EN:PDF, last consulted 17 May 2022.

courts seized of the same or related actions must or may stay proceedings.

This approach corresponds to the civil law tradition's approach to parallel proceedings, which usually operates on a first-in-time rule, while the common law tradition relies on the doctrine of *forum non conveniens*, which considers various factors to determine the appropriate forum in which to settle a dispute, including the first-in-time aspect of *lis pendens*.

Concluding remarks

The 2012 Brussels I Regulation (recast) and 2006 ILA definition of parallel proceedings both hinge on the notion of *lis pendens* and are thus both influenced by civil law. However, *lis pendens* is too narrow to capture the full complexity of parallel proceedings, and thus both definitions are found lacking.

However, the Brussels I Regulation (recast) is more modern than the ILA definition and constitutes a step forward. Whereas in the ILA definition proceedings are parallel when one or more issues are "the same or substantially the same", in the Brussels Regulation proceedings are parallel when actions are deemed to be "related", that is to say "where they are so closely connected that it is expedient to hear and determine them together to avoid the risk of irreconcilable judgments resulting from separate proceedings"[4].

The terms "related" and "connected" in the Regulation match the French term *connexes*, which better capture the full phenomenon of parallel proceedings in international arbitration. Moreover, the reference to "expedience" as a factor to determine whether proceedings are "closely connected" may be seen as a nod to the common law doctrine of *forum non conveniens*, and the ultimate aim is consistency in avoiding irreconcilable judgments. While

---

[4] See Article 30 (3) of the Brussels I Regulation (recast).

the ILA definition and the Brussels I Regulation (recast) are useful starting points, they are centred on the classic notion of *lis pendens* and are too narrow to encompass more modern scenarios, particularly in investment arbitration.

3. *A proposed modernised definition*

After reviewing past definitions and modern scenarios, it can be concluded that the term parallel proceedings broadly covers two types of situations. The first type occurs when the *same* dispute is brought before different adjudicating bodies, such as courts or tribunals. This is the classic *lis pendens* scenario, where the parties, facts and legal issues are essentially the same. The broader term "parallel proceedings" evolved from this basic matrix.

The second type of parallel proceedings involves *related* disputes that are brought before different adjudicating bodies. In this scenario, the parties may not be exactly the same, and indeed it is sufficient that at least one of the parties is common to both proceedings. The legal issues and causes of action may also vary.

The *same* disputes are by definition also *related*. Therefore, the lowest common denominator between these two major groups of parallel proceedings is that the disputes must be related. This takes us back to the French term *connexes*. The key is then to identify the nature of this connection. How do the disputes need to be related for them to qualify as parallel proceedings? Again, one must look for the lowest common denominator.

In order to qualify as parallel proceedings, two variables must be present at all times. First, at least one of the parties must be the same in both proceedings. It is often the case that the other side will also be the same party or a closely related party linked by ownership – but this is not required for "parallel proceedings" *stricto sensu*. Second, the core facts in dispute must be the same. The core facts are what define a dispute. If they are not the same, there are two different unrelated disputes. By contrast, the causes of action and legal recourses arising from these core facts may indeed differ – and very often will.

Based on these criteria, a working definition of "parallel proceedings" *in international arbitration* can be proposed as follows:

> "Parallel proceedings are two or more proceedings submitted to different adjudicating bodies, at least one of which is an international arbitral tribunal, where at a minimum:
>
> *a)* one of the parties is the same and the core facts are the same; and
>
> *b)* the proceedings are further related in the following sense:
>
> 1. both parties are the same, substantially the same, or are closely related; or
>
> 2. the causes of action are the same or substantially the same; or
>
> 3. the object of the actions are the same or substantially the same."

This definition captures the complexity behind the concept of parallel proceedings. There must be an essential core, a minimum threshold below which one cannot genuinely speak of parallel proceedings. It is the line dividing parallel proceedings from separate proceedings with similarities. But above this threshold, the concept is capable of semantic gradation and will depend on the specific circumstances of each case. The first part of the definition sets out the defining qualities of parallel proceedings, while the second part introduces the requisite degree of nuance and discretion.

The proposed definition also covers all the scenarios discussed in this course. For instance, in the field of investment arbitration, which has seen an increased focus on parallel proceedings in recent years, three of the classical scenarios are covered by this definition, viz. the scenario where claims based on contracts are brought in parallel to claims based on investment treaties, the scenario of "vertical claims", where shareholders at different levels of the same vertical corporate chain bring claims against the same State based on the same key facts or State measures, and the scenario where investors with no link of ownership between them bring claims against the same State based on the same key facts or State measures.

B. Typology of parallel proceedings

Parallel proceedings come in different types and shapes, and it is important to classify them in order to distinguish between problematic cases (for which solutions should be found) and non-problematic cases. Two classifications are proposed. The first is based on the *forum* before which the proceedings are brought. This classification is objective and allows for a systematic view of the field. The second classification, which is more subjective, is based on the *reasons* for bringing parallel proceedings.

There are two main fora where claims can be brought: international arbitral tribunals and national courts. The interaction between these two fora gives rise to four possible scenarios:

Forum	*International arbitral tribunal*	*National court*
International arbitral tribunal	*international arbitral tribunal* v. *international arbitral tribunal*	*international arbitral tribunal* v. *national court*
National court	*national court* v. *international arbitral tribunal*	*national court* v. *national court*

This matrix could be further compounded if there were more than two fora involved in the parallel proceedings; for instance, the national courts from two different jurisdictions and an international arbitration tribunal, or more than two arbitral tribunals. But, ultimately, there will always be two basic types of interactions, and this course covers these two main scenarios: national court v. international arbitration tribunal (see Chap. II) and international arbitration tribunal v. international arbitration tribunal. This second scenario can be subdivided into *(a)* purely commercial disputes with no investment arbitration element (or "commercial arbitration", see Chap. III) and *(b)* disputes with an investment arbitration element (or "investment arbitration", see Chap. IV). This course does *not* cover national court v. national court, either within the same jurisdiction or within separate jurisdictions.

There may be limitations to classifying parallel proceedings in terms of purpose, reason or motivation. After all, we cannot know with certainty the reasons why proceedings are brought in a specific case. Nor is there a closed, exhaustive list of such reasons. There could be exceptional reasons specific to a case that are beyond generic classification. Yet, despite these shortcomings, this classification is useful. If the first classification seeks to determine *what* types of parallel proceedings there are, the second tries to understand *why* such proceedings are brought. This can help us understand the root of any problems and identify possible solutions.

Parallel proceedings may be brought for several reasons. They may be brought *to secure a forum with jurisdiction*. It may be unclear what forum has jurisdiction to adjudicate the dispute. In such a case, the purpose of bringing parallel proceedings is merely to ensure that there will be a forum with jurisdiction to adjudicate the dispute. Parallel proceedings are thus used as a sort of jurisdictional insurance to minimise the risk of being left without a forum with jurisdiction to resolve the dispute. In this scenario, it is the same party – the claimant – who in principle brings the claims in different fora.

Parallel proceedings may be brought *as a result of disagreement*. Sometimes parallel proceedings can be the product of genuine, good-faith disagreement between the disputing parties. One party thinks that a particular forum has jurisdiction to settle the dispute, the other thinks it is another forum. They both have claims, and each brings its claims in the forum they believe has jurisdiction. In such a scenario, each party begins separate proceedings in good faith.

A third reason to bring parallel proceedings is *to secure a tactical advantage*. In a dispute the interests of the disputing parties are by definition on a collision course with each other. Parties often look for ways in which they can gain a tactical advantage over the other side, and parallel proceedings can be an important tool in that quest. One tactical advantage is that it may maximise the chances of success on the merits. A party bringing the same – or substantially the same – claims in more than one forum has a greater chance of winning the dispute. A claimant bringing the same claims before multiple fora only need win once, regardless of how many times it loses. This may be the most common tactical reason for a claimant to commence parallel proceedings.

A second tactical advantage relates to forum shopping. Parallel proceedings can happen because the parties shop for the forum they consider most favourable to them. They try to find a friendly forum in which to submit the claims. This can be a forum where they feel they have a "home" advantage; or where they feel they can neutralise the "home" advantage that the other side would have in another forum; or where they feel that the procedural laws or the adjudicating court or tribunal are likely to favour their position. Other factors a party might consider in forum shopping include the speed (or lack of speed) of the adjudicating bodies to decide the dispute, the costs, the seat, the language, the efficiency and support of local courts, the wish to apply for interim measures or bring counterclaims, the applicable law, and practical considerations such as the location of client, counsel team, witnesses or evidence. A third tactical advantage of bringing parallel proceedings is simply to harass the other side, for example to maximise the financial pressure on their opponent or increase the "nuisance" value of the dispute and thus the chances of settlement. In short, there is a wide array of reasons why parties bring parallel proceedings, ranging from good faith to bad faith to plain harassment, from searching for tactical advantages to maximising the chances of winning.

These two classifications thus help us address two questions: the substance of parallel proceedings (the *what*) and the reasons for bringing them (the *why*). The first classification helps us approach the subject in an orderly, methodological fashion and has intrinsic analytical value. The second classification is elusive and open-ended but more likely to help diagnose problems with the system and devise possible solutions. Both classifications accordingly complement each other well. Each serves a distinct purpose and, combined, help address both the theoretical and practical aspects of this field.

C. *Why are parallel proceedings problematic?*

Parallel proceedings present significant problems and challenges, both for the parties involved and the system of international dispute settlement as a whole. The problems are thus both case-specific or systemic. For example, the inefficiency of parallel proceedings leads to unnecessary costs and a waste of resources, as more resources need to be spent on settling the same dispute. This is especially pressing when public resources are involved, as is always the case in investment arbitration. Another problem is the potential for parallel proceedings to be used as a tool of harassment. Legal proceedings are meant to provide parties with a means to redress alleged grievances and wrongs. The potential to bring parallel proceedings over what is essentially the same alleged grievance or wrong distorts the restorative nature of a legal remedy. What is meant to be a remedy can become a weapon to harass and persecute the opposing party.

The most significant problem with parallel proceedings is the risk of inconsistent and contradictory decisions. Different adjudicating bodies can render decisions that are inconsistent or contradictory in terms of the case outcome, amount of compensation awarded, findings of fact, legal issues, and reasoning. The risk is present in both commercial and investment arbitration, but it carries greater risks and takes on a more serious dimension in investment arbitration. This is due to the nature of investment arbitration cases, which often involve State measures affecting a group of claimants (whether related or unrelated) rather than the narrower setting of parties and issues in commercial arbitration cases. Examples abound, such as the wave of cases against Argentina in relation to the financial crisis or against Spain and the Czech Republic in the renewable energy cases. State measures often involve public as opposed to commercial interests; the issues in dispute in investment arbitration cases are thus by definition more politically sensitive and the risk of contradictory decisions felt more acutely.

Parallel proceedings also pose challenges related to confidentiality, transparency, public funds, and private interests. While commercial arbitration proceedings are usually confidential, investment arbitration proceedings involving States and public interests often require greater transparency and publicity. This can be seen in the adoption of the United Nations Commission on International Trade Law ("UNCITRAL") Rules on

Transparency in Treaty-based Investor-State Arbitration, incorporated into the 2013 UNCITRAL Arbitration Rules[5], the Mauritius Convention on Transparency[6] and the proposed pro-transparency amendments of the International Centre for Settlement of Investment Disputes ("ICSID") Rules (reflected in the ICSID 2020 Working Paper No. 4)[7]. The origin of funds involved in investment arbitration are usually public (indeed, in the case of a State party, always so), making the misuse or waste of funds more concerning than in commercial arbitration cases, where the origins of the funds are usually private.

Moreover, parallel proceedings undermine the public's confidence in international arbitration as a system for resolving high-stakes disputes. The public at large, and users in particular, will inevitably lose faith in a system that is inefficient, wastes resources, can be used as a tool of harassment, and can produce inconsistent and contradictory decisions. Again, these risks are greater in the case of investment arbitration, where the involvement of the public interest, public funds and greater transparency mean these problems will be brought into sharper focus.

Despite all this, not all parallel proceedings are objectionable and only some are problematic. Some parallel proceedings are simply manifestations of a system

---

[5] The 2013 UNCITRAL Arbitration Rules, https://uncitral.un.org/sites/uncitral.un.org/files/media-documents/uncitral/en/uncitral-arbitration-rules-2013-e.pdf, last consulted 17 May 2021.

[6] The text of Mauritius Convention on Transparency, https://uncitral.un.org/sites/uncitral.un.org/files/media-documents/uncitral/en/transparency-convention-e.pdf, last consulted 17 May 2021.

[7] Working Paper #4, https://icsid.worldbank.org/sites/default/files/amendments/WP_4_Vol_1_En.pdf, last consulted 17 May 2021. These have now been incorporated into the new ICSID Rules as Arbitration Rule 62.

operating as it should. To minimise these problems, criteria must be established to distinguish between desirable and undesirable parallel proceedings. This course aims to identify undesirable parallel proceedings and propose practical solutions to address them.

D. A practical example:
Lauder *v.* Czech Republic *and*
CME *v.* Czech Republic

One of the most well-known cases of parallel proceedings in investment arbitration is the dispute involving Ronald Lauder and CME Czech Republic BV ("CME") over their investment in the Czech television channel TV Nova. Mr Lauder, a US citizen, claimed that the media council, an organ of the Czech Republic, destroyed his investment through its actions and omissions. He initiated UNCITRAL arbitration proceedings on 19 August 1999, under the United States-Czech and Slovak Republic BIT, alleging violations of several obligations, including the prohibition against arbitrary and discriminatory measures, the obligation to provide FET, the obligation to provide full protection and security, the obligation of treatment in accordance with general principles of international law, and the obligation not to expropriate unlawfully[8].

Mr Lauder's investment was made through CME, a Dutch company over which he had control. On 22 February 2000, CME initiated UNCITRAL arbitration proceedings under the Netherlands-Czech Republic BIT[9]. CME's claims were essentially the same as Mr Lauder's, including breaches of the obligation to provide

---

[8] *Ronald S. Lauder* v. *The Czech Republic*, UNCITRAL, Final Award, 3 September 2001, para. 193.
[9] *CME Czech Republic BV* v. *The Czech Republic*, UNCITRAL, Partial Award, 13 September 2001, para. 2.

FET, the obligation to provide full protection and security and the obligation not to expropriate unlawfully[10].

Despite having different tribunal members, both tribunals rendered their decisions within ten days of each other. The two decisions were diametrically opposed. The *Lauder* tribunal concluded that the Czech Republic did not violate the United States-Czech and Slovak Republic BIT, except for a minor breach regarding discriminatory and arbitrary treatment in the early days of Mr Lauder's investment[11]. The remaining dispute was deemed a private commercial dispute between Mr Lauder and his local partner[12].

In contrast, the *CME* tribunal (by majority) found that the Czech Republic breached multiple standards of protection under the Netherlands-Czech Republic BIT and ordered the country to pay CME the fair market value of the investment[13], which the tribunal later determined to be over USD 260 million[14].

---

[10] *Ibid.*, at para. 27.
[11] *Lauder*, note 8, decision at p. 74.
[12] *Ibid.*, at para. 314.
[13] *CME*, note 9, para. 624.
[14] *Ibid.*, at p. 161.

CHAPTER II

NATIONAL COURTS VERSUS INTERNATIONAL ARBITRATION TRIBUNALS

Parallel proceedings involving national courts and international arbitration are the most common type of parallel proceedings that arise in disputes submitted to arbitration, whether commercial or investment treaty disputes.

Irrespective of the theory of international arbitration one adheres to (a matter dealt with in Chapter III by reference to Professor Emmanuel Gaillard's work[15]), national courts have by default jurisdiction over any dispute that parties have not agreed to submit to arbitration. However, if parties agree to submit a dispute to arbitration, they create an exception to the default rule of national court jurisdiction. What happens if it is unclear whether the parties have agreed to submit a specific dispute to arbitration? What if it is unclear whether a specific dispute falls within the scope of an arbitration agreement?

This is one of the oldest, classical problems in international arbitration. It has the potential to give rise to parallel proceedings – and often does so. The basic consensus on how to deal with this problem is embodied in an internationally accepted principle: *competence-competence*. This principle lies at the heart of the interaction between national courts and international tribunals, and thus at the heart of this lecture.

While the principle of competence-competence is well known, there is limited consensus on its meaning

---

[15] See e.g. E. Gaillard, *Legal Theory of International Arbitration*, Leiden, Martinus Nijhoff, 2010.

and operation, which can either encourage or discourage parallel proceedings. This chapter will analyse its connection with the question of parallel proceedings, as well as two other legal devices that address the problem of parallel proceedings involving national courts: the anti-suit or anti-arbitration injunctions, and the "fork-in-the-road" clauses often used in investment arbitration.

A. Competence-competence and parallel proceedings

1. A universally accepted principle

The doctrine of competence-competence has been variously described as a "universally accepted principle"[16], "an internationally recognised standard"[17], a doctrine that "virtually all national legal systems recognize"[18]. It is typically known by two interchangeable designations: as *compétence de la competence* in French and *Kompetenz-Kompetenz* in German.

According to the competence-competence principle, understood in its "primitive form", to use the words of Professor W. W. (Rusty) Park[19], arbitral tribunals have the power to rule on their own jurisdiction whenever a party challenges it, which is necessary to ensure the efficiency and efficacy of international arbitration. Else, all a party would need do to stop proceedings and force a forum change would be to question the authority of the arbitral tribunal to adjudicate the dispute.

---

[16] C. Ferdinando Emanuele and M. Molfa, *Selected Issues in International Arbitration: The Italian Perspective*, London, Thomson Reuters, 2014, at p. 142.

[17] N. Erk-Kubat, *Parallel Proceedings in International Arbitration: A Comparative European Perspective*, The Hague, Kluwer Law International, 2014, at p. 26.

[18] G. Born, *International Commercial Arbitration*, The Hague, Kluwer Law International, 2014, at p. 1048.

[19] W. W. Park, "The Arbitrator's Jurisdiction to Determine Jurisdiction", 13 ICCA Congress Series 55 (2007), 18 March 2007.

Competence-competence thus works as an "anti-sabotage" mechanism to prevent recalcitrant and unwilling parties from derailing proceedings. As Professor Park explains:

> "In its most primitive form, the principle that arbitrators may rule on their jurisdiction serves as a measure to protect against having an arbitration derailed before it begins. The arbitral tribunal (and/or the relevant arbitral institution) need not halt the proceedings just because one side questions its authority. The principle reduces the prospect that proceedings will be derailed through a simple allegation that an arbitration clause is unenforceable, due to any number of contract law defenses. In most legal systems, arbitrators can get on with their work until ordered to stop by a judge with authority to do so." [20]

But this is only half of the story because specifying the powers of arbitral tribunals says nothing about the powers of national courts to deal with the same issues. As Professor Bermann explains:

> "All would appear to agree that Kompetenz-Kompetenz permits an arbitral tribunal to determine its own jurisdiction if it is challenged, and this of course is no minor achievement. But for this understanding, a tribunal arguably would be required to suspend proceedings whenever a party before it challenges its jurisdiction—whatever the basis of the challenge might be—and refer the jurisdictional issue to a court for determination. Allowing a party to unilaterally halt an arbitration merely by advancing a colorable reason in law why it should not go forward would dramatically impair the efficacy of arbitration.
>
> Shall we, however, infer from the fact that an arbitral tribunal *may* determine its own jurisdiction

---

[20] *Ibid.*, at pp. 6-7.

when a party challenges it that a court *may not* address that question?"[21]

The competence-competence principle thus has two different sides or effects, which must be carefully considered.

2. *The positive effect*

The competence-competence principle has two facets or effects, namely a positive effect and a negative effect. The positive effect confers on arbitral tribunals the power to rule on their own jurisdiction. It is called the "positive effect" because it is an affirmative power that enables tribunals to resolve jurisdictional challenges. This effect is universally recognised and forms a cornerstone of international arbitration. The New York Convention[22] and the ICSID Convention[23] explicitly or implicitly recognise this principle, and national arbitration laws almost universally recognise it as a foundation of international arbitration[24]. Moreover, leading arbitration rules expressly affirm the principle[25].

However, the positive effect does not address the power of national courts to rule on the jurisdiction of arbitral tribunals, which is the second facet of competence-competence, its negative effect.

---

[21] G. A. Bermann, "The 'Gateway' Problem in International Arbitration", *Yale Journal of International Law*, Vol. 37, No. 1 (2012), pp. 4-53, at p. 14.

[22] See New York Convention Article II (3).

[23] See ICSID Convention Article 41.

[24] See for instance Article 16 (1) of the UNCITRAL Model Law on International Commercial Arbitration 1985, which expressly provides that arbitral tribunals "may rule on their own jurisdiction".

[25] See for instance Article 23 (1) of the 2013 UNCITRAL Arbitration Rules, note 5: "The arbitral tribunal shall have the power to rule on its own jurisdiction, including any objections with respect to the existence or validity of the arbitration agreement."

3. *The negative effect*

The negative effect of competence-competence is not aimed at arbitral tribunals but at national courts. In cases where it applies, national courts are prohibited from ruling on the jurisdiction of an arbitral tribunal until the tribunal has had a chance to do so. Whereas the positive effect affirms the authority of tribunals to make such rulings, the negative effect restricts the ability of national courts to do so, except by way of set-aside proceedings after the tribunal has ruled on the issue.

While the positive effect of competence-competence is almost universally accepted, the negative effect has been adopted by only a few jurisdictions, including France, Switzerland and Mauritius. To appreciate the practical implications of the negative effect, it is useful to compare the current situation in France with that in England, as well as to briefly consider the approach taken in Mauritius.

French law

France is widely recognised as the leading jurisdiction on the issue of the negative effect of competence-competence. The French Code of Civil Procedure contains two key provisions: Articles 1465 and 1448. Article 1465 provides that the arbitral tribunal is the "only one" or the "exclusive one" with the power to rule on its own jurisdiction[26]. Article 1448 provides that "[w]hen a dispute subject to an arbitration agreement is brought before a court, that court shall decline jurisdiction, except if an arbitral tribunal has not yet been seized of the dispute and if the arbitration agreement is manifestly void or manifestly not applicable"[27].

---

[26] In French: "Le tribunal arbitral est seul compétent pour statuer sur les contestations relatives à son pouvoir juridictionnel."

[27] In French: "Lorsqu'un litige relevant d'une convention d'arbitrage est porté devant une juridiction de l'Etat, celle-ci

However, the reference in the French Code of Civil Procedure to the arbitral tribunal having the "sole" or "exclusive" power to rule on its jurisdiction can be misleading. As Professor Gaillard points out[28], this is not a rule of exclusivity but rather a "rule of priority". Arbitrators have priority to rule on their jurisdiction, while the French judge can revisit the question in set-aside or enforcement proceedings.

Even under French law, the negative effect of competence-competence is not absolute. French courts will decline to rule on the jurisdiction of an arbitral tribunal unless the arbitral tribunal has not yet been seized and the arbitration clause is manifestly null or inapplicable. The "manifestly null or inapplicable" threshold is very high and must be *prima facie* evident.

Ultimately, the question is whether the arbitrators should have the first say on issues of jurisdiction, with the risk that they may later be found to have been wrong, or whether the courts should pre-empt that but in a way that necessarily undermines the positive effect of competence-competence. French commentators sometimes criticise other jurisdictions that adopt a different approach as committing a sin against international arbitration, but such an attitude is both dogmatic and unfair. Nonetheless, the French approach does have one major practical advantage, which is clarity. A clear-cut choice has been made for one of the two extremes just noted, and the parties, arbitrators and courts know what to expect and how to operate the system, which can result in cost savings and efficiency.

---

se déclare incompétente sauf si le tribunal arbitral n'est pas encore saisi et si la convention d'arbitrage est manifestement nulle ou manifestement inapplicable."

[28] E. Gaillard and Y. Banifatemi, "Negative Effect of Competence-Competence: The Rule of Priority in Favour of the Arbitrators", in E. Gaillard and D. Di Pietro (eds.), *The New York Convention in Practice*, Place, Cameron May, UK, 2008, pp. 257-274, at p. 258.

English law

By contrast, the English regime is complex. It is contained in no less than five sections of the English Arbitration Act 1996 ("1996 Act"), namely sections 9, 30, 32, 67 and 72. The 1996 Act sets out rules and procedures for arbitration agreements, including the positive principle of competence-competence and the mechanism for challenging awards on jurisdiction. However, the interaction between these sections is not entirely clear, and this can lead to confusion and uncertainty.

Section 9 of the 1996 Act requires courts to stay any court action brought in breach of an agreement to arbitrate "unless satisfied that the arbitration agreement is null and void, inoperative, or incapable of being performed". Section 30 contains the positive principle of competence-competence, which allows tribunals to rule on their own jurisdiction subject to review by the courts. Section 32 provides a mechanism for parties to an arbitration or the arbitral tribunal to ask the court to determine a question of jurisdiction, subject to stringent requirements. This right can only be exercised where all parties agree or where the tribunal so directs and if that direction appears to the court likely to result in substantial time and cost savings. Section 67 of the 1996 Act provides for challenges to awards on jurisdiction, while Section 72 provides for a special mechanism whereby a party who takes no part in the arbitral proceedings may ask the court to determine issues of jurisdiction. That mechanism is not subject to any of the stringent requirements of Section 32.

The interaction between these sections is unclear, and there are some difficulties. For example, there is nothing in the wording of Section 72 to prevent a party from using that section before jurisdiction is determined by the arbitral tribunal. In *Law Debenture Trust* v. *Elektrim*[29],

---

[29] *Law Debenture Trust Corporation Plc* v. *Elektrim Finance BV & Ors* [2005] EWHC 1412 (Ch).

Mann J held that a party may indeed use Section 72 at any stage of the proceedings, including at the very outset of the case. This means that the recalcitrant party can decide who goes first and may either allow the issue to go to the tribunal (and subsequently challenge any award rendered against it under Section 67) or refuse to participate and ask the court for a final ruling under Section 72. This use of Section 72 short-circuits the stringent requirements of Section 32 and renders that section largely redundant.

Moreover, in a number of cases under Section 9 of the 1996 Act, the English courts have held that the court had a discretion, to be exercised on an *ad hoc* basis in each case as a matter of case management, whether to refer an issue of jurisdiction to the arbitrators or to decide it itself. This lack of clarity about who decides the issue can result in the need for a hearing before the court to decide who will decide the issue. In an *obiter dictum* in the *Dallah* case, Lord Collins appeared to try to clarify the position (albeit taking a step that ran directly contrary to the French position and denied any "negative effect" of competence-competence), stating that "[w]here there is an application to stay proceedings under Section 9 of the 1996 Act, both in international and domestic cases, the court will determine the issue of whether there ever was an agreement to arbitrate"[30]. Still, the lack of clarity caused by the interaction of these sections of the 1996 Act has remained in everyday practice. The overall result is one of confusion and uncertainty, which cannot be productive or desirable and can hinder the effectiveness of arbitration agreements.

Mauritian law

The International Arbitration Act 2008 ("Mauritian Act") provides an interesting example of how a new

---

[30] *Dallah Real Estate and Tourism Holding Company* v. *The Ministry of Religious Affairs, Government of Pakistan* [2010] UKSC 46, para. 97.

arbitration seat can learn from established jurisdictions. The starting point is that Mauritius has of course adopted the positive rule of competence-competence[31]. In terms of the rule of priority – that is, who goes first, the court or the arbitral tribunal – a clear choice must be made, as evidenced by this comparative study. The Mauritian legislature has opted for the French solution, where the arbitral tribunal goes first, for three core reasons.

First, this stance is likely to be perceived a pro-arbitration, which is crucial for a new arbitral seat. Second, it aligns with the general philosophy of the Mauritian Act to minimise contact points with courts during arbitral proceedings. A party arriving in Mauritius to arbitrate should not start his trip with a lengthy visit to the Mauritian courts, however pleasant the judges there. Third, the solution recommended by Professor Park in his report to the 2006 Montréal International Council for Commercial Arbitration ("ICCA") Congress, the French rule with "a summary mechanism . . . to permit courts to halt arbitral proceedings when the arbitration clause is manifestly void"[32], was in effect adopted in Mauritius, even if this was not a factor in the drafting of the Mauritian Act. Notably, the test in the Mauritian Act is framed differently to ensure that it is readily understandable to users worldwide.

Section 5 of the Act provides that all arbitration applications made to the court are to be decided by a three-judge bench of the Supreme Court, which must:

> "refer the parties to arbitration unless a party shows, on a prima facie basis, that there is a very strong probability that the arbitration agreement may be null and void, inoperative or incapable of being performed".

---

[31] See Section 20 (1) of the Mauritian Act.
[32] Park, note 19, at p. 145.

This test is substantially the same as the French test, but assessment hearing before the Supreme Court must be a summary *prima facie* and not a trial or mini-trial. Moreover, the Court may decide the issue itself where the clause is *manifestement nulle*, even when the arbitral tribunal has been constituted. This is the gloss recommended by Professor Park.

It is important to note that when the Court refers a dispute to arbitration under Section 5 of the Mauritanian Act, it is not deciding on the validity of the arbitration clause. Instead, it is finding, on a *prima facie* basis, that the party challenging the clause's validity has not demonstrated a strong probability of its invalidity. The ruling has no *res judicata* effect, and a full ruling by the Court would occur only if and when the jurisdictional award of the arbitrators is challenged later.

Although both French and Mauritian laws adopt competence-competence in its negative facet, their differences illustrate that there are more nuances than the simple dichotomy of positive and negative effect suggests. As Professor Park notes, this dichotomy simplifies what is a far more nuanced issue.

Two key factors

In international arbitration, the timing of national court intervention and the effect of the arbitral tribunal's ruling on jurisdiction are critical factors that must be considered. As Professor Park notes, courts must examine the parties' actual agreements about arbitral authority and the effect that judge gives those agreements [33].

Different approaches exist regarding when national courts can rule on the jurisdiction of an arbitral tribunal, with the American, Mauritian, and French approaches

---

[33] Park, note 19, at p. 12.

standing out. The American approach allows courts to intervene at any point (whether or not the tribunal has been seized), which leads to a high likelihood of national court intervention. The Mauritian approach permits intervention during arbitration (regardless of whether the tribunal has been seized) but only if there is a very strong possibility that the arbitration clause is null and void. This approach leads to a low likelihood of national court intervention. In the French approach, national courts cannot intervene during arbitration if the arbitral tribunal has been seized but can do so during the set-aside or enforcement proceedings. If the tribunal has not been seized, courts can intervene only if there is a manifestly null or inapplicable arbitration clause. The French approach leads to a very low likelihood of national court intervention.

Each approach has a different impact on the likelihood of parallel proceedings, with the American approach (indeed, any approach not adopting negative competence-competence) posing the highest risk of such proceedings. If the legal seat of the arbitration is unclear, it could even involve more than one national court. This results in duplication of proceedings, increased expenses, greater risk of harassment, and reduced autonomy for international arbitration. However, this approach leads to a faster final ruling on arbitral jurisdiction, fewer unwarranted arbitral proceedings, and less legitimacy concerns around arbitration proceeding without consent.

Conversely, the French approach (and those similar to it, such as the Swiss and Mauritian ones) results in a lower risk of parallel proceedings, providing greater autonomy for arbitral tribunals, less resources devoted to settling the question of arbitral jurisdiction, and less ability for one side to harass the other side. However, it leads to slower final rulings, legitimacy concerns as to arbitrating without consent, and a risk of unwarranted arbitral proceedings.

Ultimately, the allocation of jurisdiction between courts and tribunals on the issue of the tribunal's jurisdiction is part of the ordinary course of business in international arbitration. There is nothing intrinsically pathological about it. Yet the choice of which version of competence-competence to adopt does have a direct impact on the potential for and risk of parallel proceedings. Importantly, however, whatever solution is adopted, there is no risk of inconsistency. It is universally accepted that national courts are the ultimate arbiters of jurisdiction, and any determination of jurisdiction by the arbitral tribunal is subject to review by the national courts.

To minimise the risk of parallel proceedings, the obvious solution would be to adopt a negative version of competence-competence, such as the French or Mauritian version. However, only a few jurisdictions have adopted this approach to date, and the risk of parallel proceedings thus remains present in most interactions between national courts and arbitral tribunals on the question of arbitral jurisdiction.

4. *A practical example: The* Fomento *case*

The key question in the *Fomento* case[34] was whether an arbitral tribunal sitting in Switzerland should stay the arbitral proceedings, pending the decision of foreign courts on that arbitral tribunal's jurisdiction.

The case concerned a dispute between Colon Container Terminal SA ("CCT"), a Panamanian company, and Fomento de Construcciones y Contratas SA ("Fomento"), a Spanish company, arising from a 1996 contract for civil engineering works. Both parties had taken conflicting steps in the Panamanian courts and before

---

[34] Swiss Federal Tribunal, *Fomento de Construcciones y Contratas SA* v. *Colon Container Terminal SA*, ASA Bull., 2001, Vol. 3, p. 555.

an arbitral tribunal seated in Geneva, resulting in both fora being seized of the dispute. Fomento filed a claim against CCT in the Panamanian courts, prompting CCT to raise a defence asserting that the parties had agreed to resolve their disputes through arbitration. However, the Panamanian Court of First Instance dismissed this defence as being untimely. Without waiting for the proceedings in Panama to run their course, CCT commenced arbitration proceedings in Geneva under the Arbitration Rules of the International Chamber of Commerce ("ICC") and the Swiss Federal Code on Civil Procedure. Fomento subsequently challenged the jurisdiction of the arbitral tribunal. While the arbitration was ongoing, a Superior Panamanian Court reversed the decision of the First Instance Court, holding that CCT's defence was in fact timely. The arbitral tribunal in Geneva then upheld its jurisdiction, referring to the decision of the Superior Panamanian Court, without waiting for remedies to be exhausted in Panama.

However, after the award was issued, the Supreme Court of Panama reversed the decision of the Superior Panamanian Court and ordered that the dispute be heard by the courts of Panama. Fomento thus challenged the arbitral award before the Swiss Federal Tribunal, arguing that the arbitral tribunal erroneously upheld its jurisdiction by failing to stay its proceedings pending the final determination of the matter by the Panamanian courts, thereby ignoring the principle of *lis pendens* enshrined in Article 9 (1) of the Swiss Private International Law Act ("PILA")[35]. The Swiss Federal Tribunal allowed Fomento's challenge and set aside the arbitral award,

---

[35] Article 9 (1) of the Private International Law Act provides that: "If an action having the same subject matter is already pending between the same parties abroad, the Swiss court shall stay the proceeding if it may be expected that the foreign court will, within a reasonable time, render a decision that will be recognizable in Switzerland."

holding that an arbitral tribunal seated in Switzerland was (like the Swiss national courts) bound by Article 9 (1) of the PILA. The Swiss Federal Tribunal's decision was based on its understanding of the principle of *lis pendens* and its function alongside that of *res judicata* to avoid contradictory decisions.

The Swiss Federal Tribunal decided that there was no serious legal basis for granting priority to an arbitral tribunal over national courts in ruling on the tribunal's jurisdiction, and for ignoring the order of chronological priority set out in Article 9 (1) of the PILA. It mechanically applied the principle of *lis pendens*, which is "purely chronological"[36]. It thus undermined the principle of competence-competence, which is "specifically designed to protect and safeguard the arbitrators' power to rule on their jurisdiction"[37]. As a result of the *Fomento* case, the Swiss legislature added a new paragraph to Article 186 of the PILA in 2006 to clarify the application of the principle of competence-competence, stating the following:

> "The arbitral tribunal shall decide on its own jurisdiction without regard to any action having the same subject matter that is already pending between the same parties before a state court or another arbitral tribunal, unless there are substantial grounds for a stay in proceedings."[38]

B. Anti-suit (and anti-arbitration) injunctions

Competence-competence has a significant effect on parallel proceedings, increasing or reducing them indirectly. However, at its core, it is designed to allocate

---

[36] Gaillard and Banifatemi, note 28, at p. 272.

[37] *Ibid.*

[38] New Article 186, para. 1 bis, adopted by the Federal Law of 6 October 2006, which entered into force on 1 March 2007.

jurisdiction between courts and tribunals to ensure the effectiveness of arbitration as a dispute settlement method. The previous section discussed the important effects of competence-competence on parallel proceedings. The motions we now turn to, anti-suit (and anti-arbitration) injunctions and fork-in-the-road clauses, for their part are legal devices created to avoid parallel proceedings. Anti-suit injunctions have been used in commercial arbitration for a long time. By contrast, the appearance of fork-in-the-road clauses, which will be addressed in the next section, is more recent and related to the rise of investment treaties and investment arbitration.

As Professor George Bermann defines it, an anti-suit injunction is

> "an order issued by a court or tribunal at the request of one party designed to prevent another party from commencing or maintaining a legal proceeding in another forum, particularly a foreign forum"[39].

These injunctions are thus specifically devised to avoid parallel proceedings, and thus resemble *lis pendens* and *forum non conveniens* doctrines. Under *lis pendens*, a court or tribunal will defer to legal proceedings already underway in another forum. *Lis pendens*, then, essentially operates as a rule of "first in time" (i.e. first jurisdiction to be seized). It is widely accepted in civil law countries but not common law countries. Under *forum non conveniens*, a court or tribunal will defer to another forum that it deems to be more suitable (or more convenient, as the name implies) to adjudicate the dispute. While the question of whether that other forum has already been seized or not (whether it was "first in time") may be relevant to that enquiry, it is not determinative. This

---

[39] G. A. Bermann, *"Anti-Suit Injunctions*: International Adjudication", in H. Ruiz Fabri (ed.), *Max Planck Encyclopedia of International*, Oxford, Oxford University Press, 2015, at para. 1.

doctrine is widely accepted in common law countries but not civil law countries.

Both *lis pendens* and *forum non conveniens* are predicated on the self-restraint of the court or tribunal seized, whereas anti-suit injunctions are orders that purport to restrain the exercise of jurisdiction by another court or tribunal. While the restraining order is never directed at the other forum but at a party appearing before the court/tribunal passing the said order (so that it is meant to act *in personam* against that party, not as an order directly challenging the other court/tribunal), its effect is the same since it is intended indirectly to prevent that other forum from exercising jurisdiction.

Anti-suit injunctions may be issued by both courts and arbitral tribunals, and two types of injunctions can be issued, anti-suit and anti-arbitration injunctions. The matrix of possibilities is as follows:

Forum	*Anti-suit injunction*	*Anti-arbitration injunction*
National court	*(1)* Court-issued anti-suit injunction	*(3)* Court-issued anti-arbitration injunction
International arbitration tribunal	*(2)* Tribunal-issued anti-suit injunction	*(4)* Tribunal-issued anti-arbitration injunction

There may be various reasons for a court or tribunal to issue an anti-suit or anti-arbitration injunction, including to protect its own jurisdiction, comply with its own obligations (e.g. a court's obligation to refer a matter to arbitration), or protect a party's rights (e.g. the right to have a dispute settled by arbitration). Civil law jurisdictions generally do not favour these remedies as they are believed to breach international comity – that is, the deference a court or tribunal is expected to afford other courts or tribunals. As Laurent Levy, a well-known civil law arbitrator puts it, foreign adjudicators "are the arbitrator's equals and have no orders to receive"[40].

However, in common law jurisdictions, anti-suit injunctions are established remedies, and their use has been established in the United Kingdom, the United States, Australia, Canada, Hong Kong and India, where the courts have developed sophisticated case law on the matter. The most common instance of anti-suit injunctions in the arbitration context is to prevent a foreign court from taking jurisdiction over a dispute that the parties have agreed to refer to arbitration – so-called *Angelic Grace* injunctions[41]. Outside that situation, the English courts will only grant this exceptional remedy where a foreign suit can be shown to be "vexatious or oppressive"[42] – a very high threshold.

The use of anti-suit and anti-arbitration injunctions is a controversial and exceptional practice that remains at the discretion of courts and tribunals. However, their use is more acceptable in some cases than in others. In order of most acceptable to least acceptable, one could rank them as follows: *(1)* court-issued anti-suit injunctions, *(2)* tribunal-issued anti-suit injunctions, *(3)* court-issued anti-arbitration injunctions, and *(4)* tribunal-issued anti-arbitration injunctions.

The rarest form of anti-suit injunctive relief is the anti-arbitration injunction. This is because such injunctions are in direct conflict with the key principle of international arbitration we have just covered: competence-competence. Under the positive effect of competence-competence, arbitral tribunals have the power to

---

[40] L. Levy, "*Anti-Suit Injunctions* Issued by Arbitrators", Institut pour l'Arbitrage International International Arbitration Series No. 2, Paris, Juris Publishing, 2005, at p. 128.
[41] Named after the English Court of Appeal's decision in *Aggeliki Charis Compania Maritima SA* v. *Pagnan SpA (The "Angelic Grace")* [1995] 1 Lloyd's Rep. 87.
[42] See e.g. *Airbus Industries* v. *Patel* [1998] UKHL 12.

rule on their own jurisdiction. Anti-arbitration injunctions seek to restrain this power. The two are thus inevitably at odds with each other, and, as Professor Bermann notes, this is why anti-arbitration injunctions are "widely condemned"[43].

By contrast, anti-suit injunctions are more widely accepted, those issued by a court more so than those issued by a tribunal. This is because national courts – especially those bound by the New York Convention – are expected to protect the arbitration agreement and refer disputes to arbitration. Anti-suit injunctions are seen as a tool to enforce this obligation. However, the power of tribunals to issue anti-suit injunctions is contested. Those who argue in favour of the said power look to the *lex arbitri* and applicable procedural rules, and consider anti-suit injunctions as an expression of the power to issue interim measures.

In summary, anti-suit injunctions are legal devices designed to prevent parallel proceedings and to restrain the exercise of jurisdiction by another court or tribunal by ordering a party not to commence or continue proceedings. Their use remains controversial and exceptional, particularly in the case of anti-arbitration injunctions, which conflict with the principle of competence-competence. The most acceptable form of anti-suit injunctions are those aimed at other courts and not other tribunals, and which have a well-founded pro-arbitration purpose, such as protecting a party's right to arbitrate or enforcing a court's obligation to refer to arbitration. Ultimately, anti-suit injunctions remain a discretionary remedy.

C. *Fork-in-the-road clauses* (electa una via)

Investment arbitration has produced its own legal device to prevent or minimise the risk of parallel

---

[43] Bermann, note 39, at para. 40.

proceedings: fork-in-the-road ("FITR") clauses. These clauses work in one direction only: in favour of host States. They have had limited application in investor-State dispute settlement ("ISDS") practice – although it is unclear if this indicates that they do not work or that they do. FITR clauses, often included in investment treaties, such as the Energy Charter Treaty[44], typically appear in the same clause as the offer to arbitrate. They provide investors with a choice of forum for dispute resolution: the domestic courts of the host State or international arbitration (often with two or more international arbitration options on offer). Once the choice is made, the investor cannot change its mind. It is final. Hence the metaphor of the "fork in the road": the investor is at a crossroads.

The purpose of these clauses is to avoid parallel proceedings between domestic courts and ISDS tribunals. Given their often politically sensitive nature, the public funds involved and the requirement for greater transparency (see Chap. I.C), the risk of parallel proceedings are perceived as less acceptable in ISDS disputes. FITR clauses are a contrasting feature of investment arbitration compared to public international law adjudicative bodies, where exhaustion of local remedies is generally required for access to international adjudication. In investment arbitration, not only does that rule not normally apply, but where a FITR clause applies, it provides for the exact opposite: the choice of local remedies precludes access to investment arbitration.

FITR clauses are distinct from waivers of local remedies, such as that contained in Article 1121 of the old North American Free Trade Agreement ("NAFTA"). Under Article 1121 of the old NAFTA, the waiver is a condition rather than a choice for access to international arbitration. If local court proceedings are brought, that

---

[44] Energy Charter Treaty, Article 26 (3) *(b) (i)*.

does not bar access to arbitration: they can be discontinued to begin arbitration. This option is not available under a FITR clause.

Two examples of FITR clauses in investment treaties are provided by the US-Argentina and Argentina-France BITs. Article VII of the US-Argentina BIT provides:

> "2. In the event of an investment dispute . . . the national or company concerned may choose to submit the dispute for resolution:
>
> *(a)* to the courts or administrative tribunals of the Party that is a party to the dispute; *or*
> *(b)* in accordance with any applicable, previously agreed dispute-settlement procedures; *or*
> *(c)* in accordance with the terms of paragraph 3.
>
> 3. *(a)* Provided that the national or company concerned has not submitted the dispute for resolution under paragraph 2 *(a)* or *(b)* . . . the national or company concerned may choose to consent in writing to the submission of the dispute for settlement by binding [investment] arbitration." (Emphasis added)

Article 8 (2) of the Argentina-France BIT reads as follows:

> "Once an investor has submitted the dispute either to the jurisdictions of the Contracting Party involved or to international arbitration, the choice of one or the other of these procedures shall be final."

FITR clauses have been interpreted in investment case law in different ways. Most tribunals have adopted a strict interpretation of the FITR clause requiring a triple-identity test. In this test, there must exist in both sets of proceedings (before the domestic courts and before the ISDS tribunal) and identity of parties, object, and cause of action. Due to the well-established distinction between treaty and contract claims, most ISDS tribunals have dismissed claims that the FITR clause precluded a claim. Examples include *Charanne* v. *Spain*[45], *Alex Genin* v. *Estonia*[46], *Occidental* v. *Ecuador*[47] and *Toto* v. *Lebanon*[48]. In *Occidental*, the tribunal further held that the "choice" of forum by the investor must be "entirely free" and "not under any form of duress"[49]. This referred to the fact that Ecuadorian tax law required investors to file claims before local courts to stop tax assessments from becoming final.

However, some tribunals have adopted a broader "fundamental basis" test in interpreting FITR clauses. The relevant question for those tribunals is not whether there is a triple identity of parties, object, and causes of action, but whether the claims before the local courts and the ISDS tribunal have the same "fundamental basis". The leading case in this respect is *Pantechniki* v. *Albania*, where Jan Paulsson sat as sole arbitrator[50]. For this tribunal, to establish the "fundamental basis" of a claim one needed to determine whether the claims have the same "normative source"[51]. The tribunal found in that case that the claims were rooted in the same contract in both fora. In other words, the claims before the ISDS tribunal did not have "an autonomous existence outside

---

[45] *Charanne and Construction Investments* v. *Spain*, SCC Case No. V 062/2012, Award, 21 January 2016.

[46] *Alex Genin, Eastern Credit Limited, Inc. and AS Baltoil* v. *The Republic of Estonia*, ICSID Case No. ARB/99/2, Award, 25 June 2001.

[47] *Occidental Exploration and Production Company* v. *The Republic of Ecuador*, LCIA Case No. UN3467, Final Award, 1 July 2004.

[48] *Toto Costruzioni Generali SpA* v. *The Republic of Lebanon*, ICSID Case No. ARB/07/12, Decision on Jurisdiction, 11 September 2009.

[49] *Occidental*, note 47, at para. 60.

[50] *Pantechniki SA Contractors & Engineers (Greece)* v. *The Republic of Albania*, ICSID Case No. ARB/07/21, Award, 30 July 2009.

[51] *Ibid.*, at para. 62.

the contract"[52]. Other tribunals have followed this approach, namely *HH Enterprises* v. *Egypt*[53], *Supervision y Control* v. *Costa Rica*[54] and *Chevron* v. *Ecuador*[55].

---

[52] *Ibid.*, at para. 64.

[53] *H&H Enterprises Investments, Inc.* v. *Arab Republic of Egypt*, ICSID Case No. ARB 09/15, Tribunal's Decision on the Respondent's Objections to Jurisdiction, 5 June 2012.

[54] *Supervision y Control SA* v. *Republic of Costa Rica*, ICSID Case No. ARB/12/4, Final Award, 18 January 2017.

[55] *Chevron Corporation and Texaco Petroleum Corporation* v. *Ecuador (II)*, PCA Case No. 2009-23, Third Interim Award on Jurisdiction and Admissibility, 27 February 2012 *(obiter)*.

CHAPTER III

PURELY COMMERCIAL DISPUTES WITH NO INVESTMENT ARBITRATION ELEMENT

We now turn to the second category in our typology of parallel proceedings: the interaction between international arbitral tribunals in purely commercial arbitrations without an investment arbitration element. Examples of such disputes include building and insurance disputes, which often involve parallel arbitrations between various parties (e.g. project owner v. main contractor, main contractor v. subcontractor, insured v. insurer, insurer v. reinsurer).

In the court versus tribunal scenario explored in the previous chapter, the issue is *how* courts and arbitral tribunals are meant to interact and the nature, timing and sequencing of that interaction. The interaction itself is inherent to international arbitration and part of its ordinary practice. By contrast, in the tribunal versus tribunal scenario (whether commercial or investment), the issue is *whether*, and only than. Parallel proceedings between tribunals is prima facie not a normal state of affairs but an anomaly. For this reason, parallel proceedings are deemed more acceptable and less problematic in the court versus tribunal scenario than in *the tribunal* v. *tribunal scenario.* This may explain why so many jurisdictions – including major arbitral jurisdictions – are reluctant to adopt the negative facet of competence-competence.

To minimise parallel proceedings in commercial arbitration, tribunals have traditionally use many of the same legal tools as national courts, namely *lis pendens* (giving preference to the proceedings "first in time"), *res judicata* (giving binding effect to the award of one tribunal, thus discouraging parallel proceedings that might lead to inconsistent results), and the consolidation of parallel proceedings and joinder of parties into existing proceedings. However, these mechanisms cannot be simply transposed into the field of arbitration. As noted by Professor Dr Klaus Peter Berger, the cornerstone of arbitration – party autonomy and consent – are "its natural weakness [when] it comes to joinder and consolidation"[56]. The English Court of Appeal described the problem as follows in *Lincoln* v. *Sun*[57], a case dealing with questions of issue estoppel:

> "Arbitration is [in contrast to litigation] a consensual, private affair between the particular parties to a particular arbitration agreement. The resulting inability to enforce the solutions of joinder of parties or proceedings in arbitration, or to try connected arbitrations together other than by consent, is well-recognised – though the popularity of arbitration may indicate that this inability is not often inconvenient or that perceived advantages of arbitration, including confidentiality and privacy, are seen as outweighing any inconvenience. Different arbitrations on closely inter-linked issues may as a result lead to different results, even where, as in the present case, the evidence before one tribunal is very largely the same as that before the other. The arbitrators in each arbitration are appointed to decide the disputes in that arbitration between the particular parties to that arbitration. The privacy and confidentiality attaching to arbitration underline this; and even if they do not lead to non-

---

[56] OGEMID contribution of 21 January 2005, recorded i̇ M. McIlwrath and S. Moollan, "Joinder: Current Practi̇ in International Arbitration", *Trade Dispute Manageme* Vol. 3 (2005), https://www.transnational-dispute-man ment.com/article.asp?key=449.
[57] *Lincoln National Life Insurance Co.* v. *Sun Life Assur* *Co. of Canada* [2004] EWCA Civ. 1660.

parties remaining ignorant of an earlier arbitration award, they are calculated to lead to difficulties in obtaining access, and about the scope of any access, to material relating to that award[58].

. . .

The sad truth is that in the absence of any third party or consolidation procedure in arbitration, parties may be put into the position of making inconsistent cases in different proceedings. In litigation, it is possible to make inconsistent cases in the same proceedings; doing so later, in different proceedings, may come under the head of abuse of process. But that is not a reason to extend the law of issue estoppel in arbitration proceedings beyond its proper sphere."[59]

Bearing in mind these difficulties, which I will come back to later in this course, the legal tools of *lis pendens* and *res judicata* remain available in principle to manage parallel proceedings in commercial arbitration, but they typically apply when the "same parties" are involved in more than one proceeding. This is the reason why – as Antonio Crivellaro[60] has noted – these doctrines have little application in investment arbitration, where parallel proceedings usually involve different parties, even if they are affiliated (e.g. the local subsidiary, the parent ompany, a shareholder).

Each of these doctrines is considered below, before ing at the related issue of abuse of process, followed nsolidation and joinder as well as informal coor- n. Consolidation and joinder are considered in more Chapter IV, which covers cases of investment crossover, where the same underlying facts

. 68 (per Lord Justice Mance).
83 (per Lord Justice Longmore).
'Consolidation of Arbitral and Court Proceed- nt Disputes", *The Law and Practice of Inter- nd Tribunals*, Vol. 4 (2005), pp. 371-420.

can give rise to claims under commercial and investment instruments.

A. Lis pendens (lis alibi pendens)

The first available device to deal with the problem [of] parallel proceedings in commercial arbitration is [that] of *lis pendens*. This Latin expression (*litispendance* in French) has the [meaning] "lawsuit pending" or "proceedings pending". Under this doctrine, a tribunal [may] stay or suspend proceedings if the same proceedings are already pending involving the same parties and claims, before another forum.

Kaj Hober, who gave [a] course at The Hague in 2014 titled "*Res judicata* and lis pendens in international arbitration", has called the principle of *lis pendens* "a fundamental principle of procedure which is normally considered to form part of procedural public policy in most legal systems"[61]. The reference to "procedural public policy" is apt because the *lis pendens* doctrine promotes fairness and justice goals, such as preventing contradictory decisions, promoting procedural economy and efficiency, avoiding wasteful duplication of resources and protecting against harassment and abuse.

Initially developed in national court litigation, the *lis pendens* doctrine was extrapolated to international arbitration and seen as a potentially important legal device to tackle the mounting problem of parallel proceedings. In 2006, the first concerted efforts were made by the international arbitration community to tackle the

---

[61] K. Hober, "Parallel Arbitration Proceedings – Duties of the Arbitrators: Some Reflections and Ideas", in B. Cremades Sanz Pastor and J. Lew (eds.), *Parallel Sate and Arbitral Procedures*, Dossiers of the ICC Institute World Business Law Vol. 3, The Hague, Kluwer Law International, 2005, Chapter 9, pp. 242-267, at p. 253.

problem. The ILA adopted a set of "Recommendations on *Lis Pendens* and *Res Judicata* and Arbitration" pursuant to a resolution passed at its seventy-second conference meeting in Toronto [62]. That same year, a major colloquium attended by numerous high-profile arbitration practitioners was organised in Geneva, on the consolidation of proceedings in investment arbitration. To[day], fifteen years later, the issues surrounding [consolidated] proceedings in international arbitration remain, if not more so, and solutions have yet to be [found] in a meaningful way.

The ILA Recommendations pr[ovide guidance on the lis p]endens doctrine [and identify] three potential scenarios where [the]se cases [it] may be applicable. In each [case, the tribunal should proceed] with the proceedings if it should, in principle, con[tinue / contiction] pursuant to the positive [effect of competence-competence if it] determines that it has [c]ompetence. However, if parallel [effect of competence-competence] proceedings are [alr]eady underway, involving the same parties and [on]e or more identical legal issues, the ILA Recommendations identify three possible scenarios:

(a) *Tribunal* v. *Court of the seat:* The tribunal should consider a stay, taking into account the risk of annulment if the jurisdictional decisions are contradictory.

(b) *Tribunal* v. *Foreign court:* No stay is required, following the rejection of the *Fomento* case precedent.

(c) *Tribunal* v. *Tribunal:* The tribunal should generally stay the proceedings or declare that it has no jurisdiction.

It should be noted that the first two scenarios are not technically considered *lis pendens* situations because the principle of competence-competence takes priority in the interaction between courts and tribunals. In jurisdictions

---

[62] De Ly and Sheppard, note 1, at p. 83. See also Chap. I.A.2.

where negative competence-competence applies, courts will typically give priority to the tribunal's ruling on jurisdiction, and there is little risk of *lis pendens*. However, in jurisdictions that only adopt positive competence-competence, the situation is more complex. If no court has been seized, the tribunal can go ahead and rule on its own jurisdiction. But if a court has been seized, what should the tribunal do? Should it proceed to hear the case or stay its proceedings?

The ILA Recommendations provide guidance on this issue, based on the location of the court seized. The court of the seat is entitled to greater deference since it has the power to set aside the award, while foreign courts (as in the *Fomento* case) are entitled to less deference. The ILA thus recommends that tribunals should not stay proceedings if a foreign court has been seized.

Commentators hold differing views. Professor Gary Born argues that the tribunal should rule on its jurisdiction and not stay, even if the court of the seat has been seized, and even if the court of the seat has determined that the tribunal has no jurisdiction. This is because courts in other States could recognise the tribunal's award upholding jurisdiction and deny recognition of the national court judgment reaching the opposite conclusion[63]. Professor Gaillard shares this view, seeing the tribunal as part of a transnational legal order. Conversely, Professor Christophe Seraglini contends that the *Fomento* precedent should not be "dismissed outright", and that stays should be considered even where the court seized is a foreign court[64].

The theoretical outlook one takes on international arbitration may determine which position one holds. In

---

[63] Born, note 18, at p. 3783.

[64] C. Seraglini, "Brèves remarques sur les Recommendations de l'Association de droit international sur la litispendance et l'autorité de la chose jugée en abritrage", *Revue de l'Arbitrage* (2006), Vol. 4, pp. 909-925, at p. 922.

his 2007 Hague lecture on the "Aspects philosophiques du droit de l'arbitrage international", Professor Gaillard[65] proposes three alternative models for international arbitration: the territorial model, the multi-localised or Westphalian model, and the delocalised or transnational model.

The territorial model is by far the most traditional of the three. The *locus classicus* for this point of view is Doctor Francis A. Mann's 1967 article, *"Lex Facit Arbitrum"*[66]. In this long-standing debate with Professors Goldman and Fouchard about the alleged existence of an autonomous "arbitral legal order", Mann argued that this question went to the very root of arbitration: is arbitration an autonomous process created by the parties' will or is it a limited process existing solely through a State's derogation from its sovereign power to render justice? His answer was unambiguous:

> "[I]t would be intolerable if the country of the seat could not override whatever arrangements the parties may have made. The local sovereign does not yield to them except as a result of freedoms granted by himself."[67]

In other words, arbitration can only exist within the legal framework of a given State, that of its seat. It is fundamentally territorial and anchored in the national legal order of the seat. The territorial conception remains prevalent in several legal systems today, such as those of England and of most Commonwealth jurisdictions. It is also the conception most consistent with the ILA

---

[65] E. Gaillard, "Aspects philosophiques du droit de l'arbitrage international", Leiden, Martinus Nijhoff, 2008.

[66] F. A. Mann, *"Lex facit arbitrum"*, in P. Sanders (ed.), *International Arbitration: Liber amicorum for Martin Domke*, Leiden, Martinus Nijhoff, 1967, pp. 157-183.

[67] *Ibid.*, at pp. 161-162.

recommendation, giving added weight and primacy to the courts of the seat.

The multi-localised or Westphalian conception, Professor Gaillard's second model, is based on a simple idea: one of the main reasons for the existence of international arbitration as we know it today is the fact that the vast majority of countries are willing to give effect to an award under the New York Convention. On a practical level, this conception suggests that the courts of the countries where the losing party has assets and where the award will be enforced have more legitimacy to scrutinise the award than the courts of the country where the arbitration took place. In particular, they may have to assist the enforcing party with their powers of coercion. On a theoretical level, this leads one to minimise, if not altogether discard, the role of the country where the arbitration has its seat in favour of an increased role for all those countries where the award may be enforced. The arbitration is no longer localised at the seat but multi-localised at all possible places of enforcement. It exists not because the sovereign of the place of arbitration consents to its existence, but because the sovereigns of the places of enforcement are willing to recognise the binding force of its result, the award. This model is most consistent with the approach to *lis pendens* proposed by Professor Seraglini, and perhaps with that of Professor Born.

The transnational conception, Professor Gaillard's third model, disregards the parties' choice of seat as irrelevant. What matters is the parties' choice of international arbitration, which carries with it a choice of a separate and autonomous regime with its own substantive rules. These rules exist within their own autonomous legal order, an arbitral legal order disconnected from any national legal order. On a practical level, such an approach would enable an arbitrator to ignore a mandatory rule of the seat that is "out of step" with established and accepted arbitral practice. Professor Gaillard gives an example: if Ethiopia were to require its arbitrators to draft their awards on yellow paper, an international arbitrator sitting in Ethiopia would be free to draft his award on pink paper because the majority of nations would allow him to do so. This model is consistent with Professor Gaillard's approach to *lis pendens* and perhaps with that of Professor Born. While some seek to defend this model on a "natural law" basis, Professor Gaillard does not, but relies instead on the asserted premise that most States now agree on the fundamental notions that underlie international arbitration. This (transnational) conception has only found supervisory court acceptance in France.

Whichever approach is adopted, the main point remains: the two court versus tribunal settings in the ILA Recommendations are about competence-competence rather than *lis pendens*, as noted by Professor Seraglini[68]. The only setting where genuine *lis pendens* applies is in the tribunal versus tribunal setting.

There are several potential scenarios where *lis pendens* could apply in that setting, including arbitrations arising from the same arbitration agreement and arbitration rules, the same arbitration agreement but different arbitration rules, or related arbitration agreements. In the first scenario, two different tribunals are constituted under the same arbitration clause and the same arbitration rules to adjudicate the same dispute, which is a *lis pendens* scenario *stricto sensu*. The other scenarios are variations on this: the arbitration agreements are related or have a separate basis; the arbitration rules are different; and the dispute is different. While such scenarios cannot attract the application of *lis pendens stricto sensu*, it may be that one of the tribunals will draw inspiration from the Recommendations and stay their proceedings as a

---

[68] Seraglini, note 64, at p. 919.

matter of case management, although the confidentiality usually attached to commercial arbitration proceedings may render any effort at such coordination difficult in practice.

Although examples of *lis pendens* in a tribunal-tribunal context are rare, some instances include arbitration of the same dispute based on the same arbitration clause [69], separate arbitration agreements [70], or the same arbitration agreement but different disputes [71]. The ILA Recommendations continue to be influential, as demonstrated in a 2019 Paris-seated ICC tribunal award that specifically referred to them on *lis pendens* [72].

Lis pendens in a tribunal versus tribunal scenario can raise concerns about the composition of tribunals and the impartiality and independence of arbitrators where one arbitrator sits in more than one proceeding but not the others. A high-profile example of this occurred in early 2021, with the ICC disqualifying arbitrator Klaus Sachs from hearing a case on the grounds that the same party had later appointed him to also hear an overlapping

---

[69] *Italy No. 170, Tema Frugoli SpA, in liquidation (Italy)* v. *Hubei Space Quarry Industry Co. Ltd. (PR China)*, Corte di Cassazione, 1732, 7 February 2001, in A. J. Van den Berg (ed.), *Yearbook Commercial Arbitration*, Vol. 32, The Hague, Kluwer Law International, 2007, pp. 390-396.

[70] *Reading & Bates Corporation, Reading & Bates Exploration Company* v. *The Islamic Republic of Iran, National Iranian Oil Company, Iranian Marine International Oil Co.*, IUSCT Case No. 28, Interim Award (Award No. ITM 21-28), 9 June 2003.

[71] Swiss Federal Tribunal, *X. SA* v. *Y Ltd.*, 4A_210/2008, Swiss International Arbitration Law Reports, 2008, Vol. 2, No. 2.

[72] *Securiport (US) and local subsidiary* v. *Benin* (ICC tribunal seated in Paris), 28 January 2019. See report in IA Reporter, D. Charlotin, "Revealed: In Securiport v. Benin, an ICC Tribunal Finds that the Underlying Contract Does Not Contravene Data Privacy Laws, and Awards 95 Million USD in Compensation", 22 April 2020.

ICSID case based on substantially the same factual background[73].

Overall, while the doctrine of *lis pendens* is ubiquitous in national court litigation, its application in international arbitration is limited due to the few occasions where it can apply in practice. The concept of *lis pendens* at the heart of the ILA Recommendations, and the concept that seen as initially defined what parallel proceedings are, is in reality unable to cope with the main source of parallel proceedings in international arbitration, where the parties, arbitration agreements and legal bases for the claims are not quite the same.

B. Res judicata *and issue estoppel*

1. *The doctrine of* res judicata

The doctrine of *res judicata* – or claim preclusion – is another legal device used to address the issue of parallel proceedings. According to this doctrine, a dispute that has been adjudicated by an international arbitration tribunal is final and cannot be adjudicated again. This prevents re-arbitration of disputes that have already been settled, thus avoiding parallel proceedings.

Arbitral awards are typically viewed as being equivalent to national court judgments, and therefore have *res judicata* effects. However, the Final Report of the ILA Recommendations clarifies that arbitral awards should not "necessarily" be equated with judgments for the purpose of *red judicata*. This is because arbitral awards possess an international dimension that court judgments lack, and because of differences in national laws regarding the conditions and scope of the doctrine[74].

---

[73] The challenge was accepted on the basis that Sachs could prejudge issues and have access to information denied to his co-panellists. See S. Perry, "ICC Disqualifies Sachs Over Related ICSID Appointment", *Global Arbitration Review*, 12 March 2021.

[74] De Ly and Sheppard, note 1, at p. 72.

There are several reasons why *res judicata* is favoured. First, it promotes finality of the dispute, which is in the public interest. Second, it promotes efficiency by preventing duplicative proceedings. Finally, it promotes fairness by ensuring that individuals are not prosecuted twice for the same matter, as captured by the Latin maxim *ne bis in idem*.

The doctrine of *res judicata* is widely accepted and is considered a general principle of international law under Article 38 (1) *(c)* of the Statute of the International Court of Justice (ICJ), as noted by Professor Hanotiau[75]. International tribunals and commentators generally agree that it is a principle of international law, with some referring to the "sanctity" of *res judicata*[76].

Common law systems rely on case law rather than codification, but generally accept both claim preclusion *(res judicata)* and issue preclusion (issue estoppel, also referred to as "collateral estoppel" in the United States). The United States and England apply both doctrines to arbitral awards, but the US version of *res judicata* is broader than the English one, as the notion of "same claim" is more narrowly understood in English law. Furthermore, in the US, only "confirmed" awards (awards that have been recognised) are generally entitled to *res judicata* effects.

Civil law systems, on the other hand, codify *res judicata* but with a narrower understanding of the doctrine. While on paper there is no issue estoppel, in reality the *res judicata* doctrine can give preclusive

---

[75] B. Hanotiau, *Complex Arbitrations: Multi-party, Multi-contract, Multi-issue – A Comparative Study*, The Hague, Kluwer Law International, 2020, at p. 422.

[76] See *Trail Smelter Case (US v. Can.)*, 3 RIAA 1905, 1949-50 (1941). For further authority, see e.g. Gaillard, "Coordination or Chaos: Do the Principles of Comity, *Lis Pendens* and *Res Judicata* Apply to International Arbitration?", *American Review of International Arbitration*, Vol. 29, No. 3, 2018, pp. 205-242, at p. 205, at n. 97 (p. 225).

effect to parts of the reasoning of an award. In French law, awards have *res judicata* effects from the moment they are issued. Article 1484 of the French Code of Civil Procedure (applicable to international arbitration via Art. 1506) provides that "the arbitral award has, as soon as it is rendered, res judicata effect with respect to the disputes it settles"[77]. In German law, Article 1055 of the German Code of Civil Procedure provides: "The arbitral award has the same effect between the parties as a final and binding court judgment." Similar provisions can be found in Dutch[78], Austrian[79] and Swiss[80] law.

Article III of the New York Convention provides that Contracting States "shall recognise arbitral awards" as "binding". The *res judicata* effects of New York Convention awards derive from this provision, as the binding nature of an award prevents re-arbitration of the matter. Similarly, Article 35 (1) of the UNCITRAL Model Law provides that arbitral awards shall be recognised as "binding" regardless of where they were made, and *res judicata* effects follow from this attribute. The binding effect of awards is also expressed in Article 34 (2) of the 2013 UNCITRAL Arbitration Rules and in Article 53 (1) of the ICSID Convention.

2. *The conditions for the application of* res judicata *to international arbitral awards*

Although there are variations across different legal systems, the 2006 ILA Recommendations on *Res Judicata* outline four elements that are generally agreed upon and must be met cumulatively. These are:

---

[77] In French: "La sentence arbitrale a, dès qu'elle est rendue, l'autorité de la chose jugée relativement à la contestation qu'elle tranche" (emphasis added).

[78] Article 1059 of the Dutch Code of Civil Procedure.

[79] Article 594 of the Austrian Code of Civil Procedure.

[80] Article 190 of the PILA.

(*a*) The award must be final and binding, with no impediment to recognition in the country where subsequent arbitration may take place.

(*b*) The award must have decided a claim for relief that is sought or is being re-argued in the further arbitration proceedings.

(*c*) The claims must arise from the same cause of action.

(*d*) The parties involved in the subsequent arbitration must be the same as those in the original award[81].

Therefore, the *res judicata* doctrine typically employs a triple-identity test, requiring that the parties, cause of action and claims must be the same. This test is similar to the triple-identity test used in the context of FITR clauses (see Chap. II.C), which tribunals have effectively imported from the *res judicata* doctrine.

Res judicata has both positive and negative effects, much like the doctrine of competence-competence (see Chap. II.A.2-3):

(*a*) The positive, or conclusive, effects of the doctrine mean that the award is final and binding and must be complied with in good faith.

(*b*) The negative, or preclusive, effects of the doctrine mean that the claims and issues cannot be relitigated or re-arbitrated.

The 2006 ILA Recommendations on *Res Judicata* recognise both the conclusive and preclusive effects:

(*a*) The conclusive effect of the arbitral award includes the dispositive part of the award (decisions and findings), its "necessary reasoning", and issues of fact or law that were "essential or fundamental to the dispositive part of the award"[82].

---

[81] De Ly and Sheppard, note 1, at p. 85.

[82] Note: This shows that the ILA Recommendations also recognise issue estoppel.

(b) The ILA recommends that the preclusive effects extend not only to the claims actually decided in the award, but also to the claims "which could have been raised" but were not, provided that raising any such claims constitute "abuse" or "unfairness"[83].

It is important to note that the *res judicata* doctrine does not only cover final awards, but also final decisions on discrete aspects of the dispute, such as jurisdiction or liability.

In summary, under the ILA Recommendations, *res judicata* covers the dispositive part of the award, necessary reasoning, and necessary issues of fact or law for the decisions, claims decided, and claims that could have been brought but were not, and final awards and final decisions on separate aspects of the dispute.

C. *The related doctrine of abuse of process*

In addition to res judicata and issue estoppel, with the stringent requirements of the triple identity test, common law jurisdictions have long developed a more flexible tool to deal with situations not falling precisely within that test. In particular, it has long been established that, in certain circumstances, a party may not seek to relitigate with a third-party, issues already litigated and determined in prior litigation in which it was involved and may not bring a new suit to litigate issues connected to prior litigation which ought to have been brought and tried in that prior litigation. The below extracts from English court decisions show the manner in which the principle has been articulated:

In *Bragg* v. *Oceanus Mutual*, Lord Justice Kerr noted that

"it is clear that an attempt to relitigate in another action issues which have been fully investigated and

---

⁸³ De Ly and Sheppard, note 1, at p. 85.

decided in a former action may constitute an abuse of process, quite apart from any question of res judicata or issue estoppel on the ground that the parties or their privies are the same"[84].

In *Arthur JS Hall* v. *Simons*, Lord Hoffmann held:

"The law discourages relitigation of the same issues except by means of an appeal. The Latin maxims often quoted are nemo debet bis vexari pro una et eadem causa and interest rei publicae ut finis sit litium. They are usually mentioned in tandem but it is important to notice that the policies they state are not quite the same. The first is concerned with the interests of the defendant: a person should not be troubled twice for the same reason. This policy has generated the rules which prevent relitigation when the parties are the same: autrefois acquit, res judicata and issue estopp' The second policy is wider: it is concerned with interests of the state. There is a general public i' in the same issue not being litigated over ag' second policy can be used to justify the ex' the rules of issue estoppel to cases in whic' are not the same but the circumstances bring the case within the spirit of the '

In *Johnson* v. *Gore Wood*, Lord B' considered an alleged abuse of th' *Henderson* v. *Henderson* and held'

"*Henderson* v. *Henders'* now understood, although' cause of action estop' much in common wit' interest is the same'

____

[84] *Bragg* v. *Oceanus* p. 137.
[85] *Arthur JS Hall* 701 A-C.

litigation and that a party should not be twice vexed in the same matter. This public interest is reinforced by the current emphasis on efficiency and economy in the conduct of litigation, in the interests of parties and the public as a whole. The bringing of a claim or the raising of a defence in later proceedings may, without more, amount to abuse if the court is satisfied (the onus being on the party alleging abuse) that the claim or defence should have been raised in the earlier proceedings if it was to be raised at all."[86]

The doctrine of abuse of process applies to protect the finality of arbitral awards just as it does to protect the finality of court judgments[87]. However, there are practical difficulties with the operation of the doctrines of *res judicata*, issue estoppel and abuse of process in relation to arbitral awards. The case of *Lincoln* v. *Sun* demonstrates further practical limits to the use of these doctrines. The Court of Appeal's judgment acknowledges that there may be little one can do to stop parallel proceedings in arbitration given its consensual nature and the practical difficulties arising from the confidentiality of arbitral awards (which will mean that the award from which preclusive effect is said to often not be known to the third party, nor be in the later proceedings).

of cases where *res judicata* arose, include based on the same arbitration clause: v. *Hubei Space Quarry*[88], two ICC

[87] *...ood & Co* [2002] 2 AC 1. *Henderson* v. *Hare* 100) (at p.31A-E). Other members *...*ittee agreed with Lord Bingham.

[88] *... Partners Limited* v. *Sinclair* [2017]

...goli SpA, in liquidation (Italy) v. *...stry Co. Ltd. (PR China)*, Corte *...*bruary 2001, in A. J. Van den

arbitrations: Nos. 2475 and 2762[89], and an ICSID case: *Southern Pacific* v. *Egypt*[90].

D. *Consolidation and joinder/intervention*

As noted at the beginning of this course, are considered at this juncture by reference to the topics of consolidation, joinder and intervention to both commercial and investment arbitration given their relevance in both fields. International commercial transactions often involve multiple parties, leading to multiparty disputes that create challenges in international arbitration. Such disputes can lead to parallel proceedings, which pose some of the most challenging issues in international arbitration, such as extension of the arbitration agreement to non-signatories, group of companies or assignments. To address parallel proceedings in a multiparty scenario, the two main tools are consolidation and joinder, with intervention being the flipside of joinder.

Consolidation refers to fusing two or more proceedings into a single proceeding. In joinder, the parties to an arbitration A and B seek to add C to the proceedings, a classic scenario coming from the building construction sector, where the principal and main contractor may seek to add the subcontractor to the proceedings. Intervention is the same scenario as joinder, except that it is C that seeks to be added to the proceedings.

The main advantages of consolidation and joinder are efficiency, saving legal resources and a lower or no risk of inconsistent decisions. However, they also pose unique problems, notably with the composition of

---

Berg (ed.), *Yearbook Commercial Arbitration*, Vol. 32, The Hague, Kluwer Law International, 2007, pp. 390-396.

[89] S. Jarvin and Y. Derains (eds.), *Collection of ICC Arbitral Awards 1974-1985*, 1990, at p. 325.

[90] *Southern Pacific Properties (Middle East) Limited* v. *Arab Republic of Egypt*, ICSID Case No. ARB/84/3, Decision on Jurisdiction, 14 April 1988.

arbitral tribunals. In the classic two-party arbitration, each party appoints one party-appointed arbitrator, with the president nominated jointly or by a neutral appointing authority. However, in uneven sides scenarios such as one claimant and two respondents, the two parties on the same side may have to "share" an arbitrator. This was the case in the *Dutco* saga, where the ICC required two co-respondents to appoint the same arbitrator, failing which the ICC Court would appoint one. The French Cour de Cassation deemed that the tribunal had been irregularly constituted and that this breached equality[91]. As a result of *Dutco*, the ICC amended its rules in 1998, giving the ICC Court the power to appoint all members of the tribunal in multiparty arbitrations. Since 2017, the ICC Rules also provide a rule for the joint nomination of one arbitrator in cases of multiparty arbitrations, whether there are multiple claimants or multiple respondents. In that way, the same rule applies *ex ante* to both sides and the inequality noted by the French court in *Dutco* is averted.

However, the main obstacle to consolidation, joinder and intervention in arbitration is the cardinal requirement of the *consent* of all parties involved. The term "consolidation" covers different situations, strictly referring to the joinder of two or more claims already pending before different tribunals, and in a broader and loose sense, used to refer to the constitution of a single tribunal to hear multiple claims from different parties for the first time. In this broader sense, there is no real consolidation of claims before different tribunals, but rather an aggregation of claims before a single tribunal from the outset. Thus, a distinction should be drawn between consolidation proper and aggregation of claims.

---

[91] C. Cass 1re, Pourvois Nos. 89-18.708 and 89-18-726, 7 January 1992.

In the investment arbitration field, the practice of *de facto* aggregation of claims pending determination of questions of consent by the appointed tribunal has taken root and is consistently used in the context of ICSID. The aggregation of claims can take one of two forms. The claims may be fully aggregated, resulting in a single award ("full aggregation"), or simply heard concurrently, resulting in separate awards ("partial aggregation"). Whether aggregation is full or partial, there is from the outset and at all times a single tribunal and single proceeding – a key distinction from consolidation proper.

The (now superseded) NAFTA was the first investment treaty to address the question of consolidation systematically. Under Article 1117 (3), consolidation was the default rule in the event of multiple claims from related investors: claims "arising out of the same events . . . should be heard together by" the same tribunal. NAFTA was thus a pioneering investment treaty in this area.

Article 11-26 of NAFTA was the focal provision on consolidation and in instructive for two reasons. First, it serves as an archetypal example of a consolidation provision in an investment treaty, with the rare benefit of some interpreting case law, in the form of the decision in *Corn Products*[92] and *Canfor*[93]. Second, it offers a useful model for how consolidation should operate in practice, whether in an investment treaty, institutional rules or national laws.

Article 11-26 of NAFTA highlights two key prerequisites for any sound consolidation provision: *(a)*

---

[92] *Corn Products International, Inc.* v. *United Mexican States*, ICSID Case No. ARB (AF)/04/1 and *Archer Daniels Midland Company and Tate & Lyle Ingredients Americas, Inc.* v. *The United Mexican States*, ICSID Case No. ARB (AF)/04/5, Order of the Consolidation Tribunal, 20 May 2005.

[93] *Canfor Corporation* v. *United States of America*; *Tembe* et al. v. *United States of America*; *Terminal Forest Products Ltd.* v. *United States of America*, UNCITRAL, Order of the Consolidation Tribunal, 7 September 2005.

the disputing parties must provide *ex ante* consent to consolidation before a dispute arises, thereby obviating the need for *ex post* consent when tactical or other considerations may mean it will not be forthcoming; and *(b)* a workable mechanism must be in place to enable consolidation even in the face of opposition. Article 11-26 does both. First at provides that a disputing party can request consolidation with other NAFTA claims "that have a question of law or fact in common". A party contracting into the regime thus explicitly accepts the risk *ex ante* that consolidation may be ordered against its post-dispute wishes. Secondly, it enables consolidation even where opposed through the establishment of a "super-tribunal" [94] to hear consolidation requests and divest previously constituted tribunals of their jurisdiction, either partially or completely, as well as stay proceedings pending its decision.

These prerequisites can be addressed at various levels, depending on the context. The highest level is including them in the treaty that creates the parties' right and duty to arbitrate. In the commercial sphere, they can be set out in the parties' specifically negotiated arbitration clause, in the chosen arbitration rules, or in the *lex arbitri*, which may provide for consolidation or joinder by tribunals or the court.

Starting with specific arbitration clauses there is anecdotal evidence of very long and complex clauses negotiated, for instance, in building projects, but this approach is not feasible for most situations and Pras the disavantage of recording the prerequisites of *ex ante* consent and practical means at the lowest possible level. For those to apply, the relevant party must be a contracting party to the specific agreement or agreements.

---

[94] This expression is not actually found in NAFTA but has been used by commentators. It was coined by Jan Paulsson in "Arbitration Without Privity", *ICSID Review*, Vol. 10., No. 2 (1995), pp. 232-257, at p. 248.

As for, arbitration rules examples include the Arbitration Rules 2014 of the London Court of International Arbitration ("LCIA") (at Art. 22 (1) *(viii)-(x)*) and the ICC Arbitration Rules (at Art. 7 on joinder and Art. 10 on consolidation). Example of *Lex arbitri* containing relevant provisions are section 2 of Schedule 2 of the New Zealand Arbitration Act 1996 or Section 3B and Schedule 1 of the Mauritian Act. In US law, following the landmark decision of *Nereus* in 1975, it used to be the case that courts could order consolidation in the absence of parties' consent [95]. But *Nereus* is no longer good law: parties must consent to consolidation [96].

In practice, both arbitral institutions and courts have ordered or refused consolidation and joinder. For instance, despite the requirements of Article 4 (6) of the 1998 ICC Rules being met, the ICC Court refused the consolidation of two arbitrations between the same parties where the arbitration clauses in each of the contracts had different seats, one Paris, the other, Amsterdam. For the ICC Court, this showed that the parties had intended to conduct separate arbitrations [97]. Yet, in a different case, the same court did order consolidation where it deemed that the arbitrations were part of the same "legal relationship" and the terms of reference had not yet been signed or approved by the court [98]. The Swiss Federal Tribunal ordered the consolidation of a dispute based on related contracts with differently worded arbitration clauses in *Andersen Consulting* v. *Arthur Andersen* [99]. Joinder was ordered by an UNCITRAL *ad hoc* tribunal

---

[95] *Compania Espanola de Petroleos, SA* v. *Nereus Shipping*, 527 F.2d 966 (2d Cir. 1975).

[96] Born, note 18, at p. 2577.

[97] Hanotiau, note 75, at pp. 182-184.

[98] *Ibid.*, at pp. 182-184.

[99] *Andersen Consulting Business Unit Member Firms* v. *Arthur Andersen Business Unit Member Firms*, Case No. 9797/CK/ AER/ACS ICC, interim award of 29 April 1999, unpublished. The Swiss Federal Court decision of 8 December 1999

in an unpublished award of 3 March 1999[100] and in a published award of 27 October 1989[101].

E. Informal coordination?

Finally, it is worth considering whether informal methods can be used to prevent or mitigate the risks of inconsistency associated with parallel proceedings'. One potential approach would be for tribunals to share information about their respective proceedings or to coordinate their hearings informally. However, in the realm of commercial arbitration, this is challenging without the parties' consent, which is, as stated above, typically not given *ex post*. Moreover, each proceeding is likely to be subject to confidentiality obligations, which can hinder coordination efforts, as noted by Lord Justice Mance (as he then was) in *Lincoln* v. *Sun*. In the next chapter, we will explore how the growing transparency in the investment arbitration arena could allow coordination to become a more effective tool for tribunals and parties, manage parallel proceedings.

---

dismissing the action to set aside is published in 18 ASA Bull. 546 (2000).

[100] Hanotiau, note 75, at p. 167.

[101] *Marine Drive Complex* v. *Ghana*, Award of 27 October 1989, 19 YB Com. Arb. 11 (1994), at 17-18.

CHAPTER IV

DISPUTES WITH AN INVESTMENT
ARBITRATION ELEMENT

The third and final category in our typology of parallel proceedings is disputes that include an investment arbitration component, the second sub-group of the tribunal v. tribunal type. Just as with the first sub-group, in commercial arbitration, the *tribunal* v. *tribunal* interaction in investment arbitrations does not represent a normal state of affairs. Investment tribunals are not designed to work in tandem the way courts and tribunals are. However, there are important differences between these two sub-groups. First, there are unique sources of parallel proceedings in investment arbitration, making the issue of parallel proceedings more severe in investment than in commercial arbitration. Second, investment arbitration involves States or state entities, making the issue of parallel proceedings more pressing as it involves public funds and more visible as investment arbitrations are often publicised.

It is therefore no surprise that the hallmark case of parallel proceedings, *Lauder/CME* v. *Czech Republic*, is an investment case covered in the first chapter (sec. D). The case exposed the glaring inconsistencies of two high-profile tribunals, resulting in two diametrically opposed outcomes for the *same* dispute. In one instance, the Czech Republic was found not to be liable, while in the other, it was found liable for hundreds of millions of euros. This is an outcome no legal system fit for purpose should allow and highlights the need for effective management of parallel proceedings in investment arbitration.

A. *Investment arbitration, a fertile ground for parallel proceedings*

The *Lauder/CME* case was just one of many investment arbitrations that occurred in the first decade of the twenty-first century. The Argentine crisis of 2001 resulted in dozens of investment arbitrations over the same State measures (the so-called *pesificación* of the tariffs of foreign-owned utilities and other tariffs that had been calculated in US dollars). This generated significant academic activity, including articles, seminars and events.

The prologue to the 2006 Final Report on the Geneva Colloquium on Consolidation of Proceedings in Investment Arbitration observed that "Argentina's financial crisis is the foremost recent illustration of [the] phenomenon [of parallel proceedings]"[102]. It added that the crisis had "generated 37 ICSID arbitrations"[103]. Even with fifteen years of hindsight, this is still a very heavy caseload to emerge from the same crisis. Crises in other countries likewise spawned scores of investment claims. United Nations Conference on Trade and Development data indicates that Argentina has been the most frequent respondent in investment arbitration with sixty-two cases[104], followed by Venezuela (fifty-four), Spain (fifty-three), the Czech Republic (forty-one) and Egypt (forty)[105].

---

[102] G. Kaufmann-Kohler *et al.*, "Consolidation of Proceedings in Investment Arbitration: How Can Multiple Proceedings Arising from the Same or Related Situations be Handled Efficiently?: Final Report on the Geneva Colloquium held on 22 April 2006", *ICSID Review: Foreign Investment Law Journal*, Vol. 21, No. 1 (2006), pp. 59-125, at p. 63.

[103] *Ibid.*

[104] UNCTAD, Investor-State Dispute Settlement Cases: Facts and Figures 2020, Issue 4, September 2021, Appendix 2, https://unctad.org/system/files/official-document/diaepcb inf2021d7_en.pdf, last consulted 25 May 2022.

[105] *Ibid.*

There are three key reasons why investment arbitration is more prone to parallel proceedings than commercial arbitration. First, the factual matrix of investment claims often involve contracts that have their own arbitration clauses. Second, investment arbitration can lead to multiple investors from the same corporate chain making separate claims against the same State over the same dispute (the problem of "vertical claims"). Lastly, a single State measure can give rise to multiple claims in arbitration from different investors with no links of ownership. These three sources of parallel proceedings in investment arbitration will be explored in depth in sections B.1, B.2 and B.3 below.

These three scenarios will not routinely arise in commercial arbitration. First, in commercial arbitration there is typically one normative source for claims – contracts. No question will arise over how a public international law claim under a treaty and a contract claim should interact. Second, in commercial arbitration there is no real risk of vertical claims: the contract will have one or more parties on each side, and claims will typically be brought by one set of parties against another within the same arbitration. Questions may arise as to whether a non-signatory to the contract is also bound by the arbitration clause (potentially raising issues such as the application of the "group-of-companies" doctrine), but those will typically be resolved by the mandated tribunal (or a national court where negative competence-competence does not operate). By contrast, vertical claims are about linked claimants bringing separate claims against the same respondent, often under different treaties.

Finally, in commercial arbitration it would be unusual for a single action by a party to result in a wave of separate arbitrations from unrelated claimants. By contrast, a single State measure can give rise to just such a scenario – as happened in the investment arbitration sagas involving Argentina, Spain, the Czech Republic, Ecuador and Venezuela, where a single State measure affected a whole class of investors. The only scenario that bears a resemblance in commercial arbitration is contracts of adhesion where one side dictates all of the contract terms, for example in consumer and employment contracts. But there are important differences between these two scenarios: investment arbitration claims are usually high in value and thus can be brought as standalone claims, whereas contracts of adhesion claims – from consumer or employment contracts – are often low in value and thus unviable as a standalone arbitration claim; many legal systems in fact prevent or regulate arbitration of consumer contracts, and in investment arbitration the investor has a range of options to bring claims – to national courts or arbitration under different treaties and different rules – that are absent in adhesion contracts.

These three scenarios of investment arbitration share a common characteristic: they are all expressions of what Jan Paulsson famously referred to as "arbitration without privity" more than a quarter of a century ago [106]. In investment arbitration, States extend open-ended arbitration offers to an open-ended class of "investors", and this has a number of consequences. The first is that investors who have signed contracts with the State can also rely on these treaties as a source for claims. The second is that investors who are part of the same corporate chain can bring separate vertical claims over the same measure or facts. And the third that, a single State measure can affect the treaty rights of an entire class of unrelated investors, leading to a wave of investment claims.

This makes investment arbitration fundamentally different from commercial arbitration. As Jan Paulsson

---

[106] Paulsson, note 94, at pp. 232 *et seq.*

noted in 1995, investment arbitration is not just a "subgenre of [the] existing discipline [of commercial arbitration]"[107]. Rather, treaty-based investment arbitration is "dramatically different from anything previously known in the international sphere"[108]. This dramatic difference – which remains to this day – lies at the root of the problem of parallel proceedings in investment arbitration. It explains why this problem is far more acute in this field, and why traditional solutions from commercial arbitration – *lis pendens*, *res judicata*, post-dispute consolidation – have been even less effective in addressing the issue in this field.

On the undesirability scale – recalling the *why* classification from the first chapter (sec. B) – parallel proceedings against States, particularly if perceived as abusive or unfair, rank high. Two main reasons underlie this. First, on the side of States (or at least some of them), there is a sense that States may not have fully understood the potential implications of investment treaties when they signed up to them, as Jan Paulsson pointed out when the field was still in its early stages. He noted in his seminal article of 1995 that "many [national governments] may not have appreciated the full implications of the new treaty obligations [in investment treaties]"[109]. Second, on the side of investors (or at least some of them), there is a sense that they should be free to use a system built for them in whichever way works best for them, which contrasts with some States' view that such use should be limited in certain circumstances because, by bringing parallel proceedings, investors are abusing the system to their advantage and to the detriment of States.

These and other features have led to a so-called "backlash" against investment arbitration, with some States withdrawing from the ICSID Convention: Bolivia

---

[107] *Ibid.*, at p. 256.
[108] *Ibid.*, at p. 256.
[109] *Ibid.*, at p. 257.

in 2007, Ecuador in 2009 (a decision reversed in 2021) and Venezuela in 2012. As noted by Walid Ben Hamida[110], the issue of parallel proceedings has played a significant role in this development, and it is also central as the calls for reform which havec since been made within the UN system, particularly at UNCITRAL, which I will discuss in the final chapter.

This highlights the importance of addressing the issue of parallel proceedings in investment arbitration. If the future of investment arbitration depends on how countries view this field, and if parallel proceedings have the potential to negatively impact these views, then it is crucial for the system to effectively tackle this problem.

B. Sources of parallel proceedings in investment arbitration

1. Contract claims v. treaty claims

The interrelationship between contract claims and treaty claims has long been a fundamental and disputed issue in investment arbitration, as noted by Professor James Crawford in 2008[111]. Before the widespread use of investment treaties, foreign investors and host States would articulate investments through agreements such as contracts, licences, concessions, permits and authorisations, creating a direct legal relationship or "privity" between them, giving rise to contract-based claims. Investment treaties did not put an end to this,

---

[110] W. Ben Hamida, "L'arbitrage Etat-Investisseur face à un désordre Procédural: La concurrence des procédures et les conflits de juridiction", *Annuaire Français de Droit International* (2005), pp. 564 *et seq.*

[111] J. Crawford, "Treaty and Contract in Investment Arbitration", *Arbitration International*, Vol. 24, No. 3 (2008), pp. 351-374, at p. 351.

but rather provided an additional layer of protection to foreign investors in the form of treaty claims[112].

Of course, a foreign investor may be protected under an investment treaty even if no contract with the host State exists (many protected investments do not involve a direct legal relationship with the State). But when a contractual relationship does exist, the investment treaty adds an extra layer of protection, typically in the form of treaty standards of treatment and access to international arbitration, leading to questions about how the two layers and their respective proceedings should interact. The interplay between contract and treaty claims has been one of the most difficult legal issues faced by arbitral tribunals in the first decade of this century, during the expansion of investment arbitration, though these are not entirely novel legal issues.

The duality of contract and treaty claims is a significant cause of parallel proceedings in investment arbitration for two reasons: *(a)* they are rooted in independent, normative sources and *(b)* in investment arbitration, unlike general international law, there is no rule of exhaustion of local remedies.

Contracts and treaties are considered to be independent normative sources. Claims arising from contracts are – typically like the contracts themselves – rooted in national law, while treaty claims are based on an international agreement, such as the BIT or other international investment agreements. As a result, each of them gives rise to separate claims, often in distinct fora. Although the distinction between contract and treaty claims is now widely considered to be *jurisprudence constante* (to the extent it can be called such, as there is no doctrine of precedent properly speaking in investment arbitration), this was not always the case. The decision of the ICSID *ad hoc* Committee in *Vivendi* v. *Argentina*

---

[112] *Ibid.*, at p. 374.

("Vivendi I") [113] has had a significant impact in this regard.

In *Vivendi I*, the claimants brought ICSID arbitration proceedings against Argentina under the Argentina-France BIT, without having recourse first to the local courts of Tucuman, Argentina, where they had entered into a Concession Contract to operate a water and sewage system. The Concession Contract had a dispute resolution clause providing for the "exclusive jurisdiction" of the Tucuman courts. The claimants argued that the province had undermined their operation of the concession (the "Tucuman claims") and that Argentina had failed to rein in the conduct of the Tucuman authorities (the "federal claims").

The tribunal upheld its jurisdiction over the BIT treaty claims but dismissed the claims on the merits, stating that it was "impossible" to separate the treaty claims from the contract claims [114]. The tribunal held that both claims were related to the performance of the contract, and that the contract provided an exclusive forum for such questions: thus, the claimants had a "duty" to pursue these claims before the courts of Tucuman. It dismissed the claims without examining them further on the merits. The *ad hoc* Committee annulled the tribunal's decision on this point [115].

The *ad hoc* Committee drew a distinction between the two claims, stating that "[a] state may breach a treaty without breaching a contract, and *vice versa*" [116]. In drawing this distinction, it relied on Article 3 of the International Law Commission's Articles on State responsibility, which provides that "The characterization of an act of a State as internationally wrongful is

---

[113] *Compañiá de Aguas del Aconquija SA and Vivendi Universal SA* v. *Argentine Republic*, ICSID Case No. ARB/97/3.
[114] *Ibid.*, Award, 21 November 2001, at p. 3.
[115] *Ibid.*, Decision on Annulment, 3 July 2002.
[116] *Ibid.*

governed by international law. Such characterization is not affected by the characterization of the same act as lawful by internal law". The Committee held that the Concession Contract's provision of local court jurisdiction did not deprive the BIT tribunal of its separate treaty jurisdiction, since the two were distinct. The ICSID tribunal would not have exercised contract jurisdiction but would instead have taken into account the contract to decide if there was a breach of the BIT. The tribunal had the duty to consider whether there was a breach of the BIT – but failed to do so; and the decision was annulled on this point. Professor Christoph Schreuer has called this decision "the most important case" on the relationship between treaty and contract [117].

Two investment tribunals faced similar issues of treaty v. contract in two well-known cases shortly after *Vivendi I*. In *SGS* v. *Pakistan*, the Swiss company Société Générale de Surveillance entered into a contract with Pakistan to provide pre-shipment inspection services for goods to be exported from certain countries to Pakistan. The contract had a forum selection clause providing for the resolution of disputes under the contract by way of domestic arbitration in Islamabad. A dispute arose under the contract. Pakistan began domestic arbitration under the contract; then SGS started ICSID arbitration under the Switzerland-Pakistan BIT. Pakistan objected to the ICSID claims arguing that the domestic arbitrator had "exclusive jurisdiction" over the dispute. The ICSID tribunal upheld its jurisdiction on the ground that it was

---

[117] C. Schreuer, "Investment Treaty Arbitration and Jurisdiction over Contract Claims: The Vivendi I Case Considered", in T. Weiler (ed.), *International Investment Law and Arbitration: Leading Cases from the ICSID, NAFTA, Bilateral Treaties and Customary International Law*, Place, Cameron May, 2005, pp. 281-323, at p. 281.

treaty jurisdiction, thus to be distinguished from contract jurisdiction [118].

In the case of *SGS* v. *Philippines*, SGS again entered into a contract for pre-shipment inspection services, this time with the Philippines. The contract contained a forum selection clause in favour of domestic courts. When a dispute arose over whether certain payments were due under the contract, SGS filed an ICSID claim. The Philippines objected based on the forum selection clause, but the tribunal upheld its jurisdiction and decided to stay the arbitration pending a decision "in the agreed contractual forum" [119]. Unlike in *Vivendi I*, the claims were not dismissed, but rather the case was stayed.

Investment claims are thus prone to parallel proceedings because they often involve a contractual aspect, leading to dual legal sources for claims: contract and treaty. These may provide for different fora for dispute resolution, such as a tribunal and a court (as in *Vivendi I* and *SGS* v. *Philippines*), or two different tribunals (domestic and international, as in *SGS* v. *Pakistan*, or international and international). Even if both the treaty and contract provide for the same dispute resolution mechanism, say ICSID, a claimant may still request the establishment of two separate tribunals to adjudicate each dispute, as explained by Walid Ben Hamida:

> "On ajoute qu'à suivre les directives jurisprudentielles, dans l'hypothèse où le contrat et le traité se réfèrent aux mêmes mécanismes arbitraux, le demandeur peut demander l'établissement de deux tribunaux arbitraux différents. Ainsi, à titre d'exemple, si le contrat d'investissement renvoie au CIRDI et

---

[118] *SGS Société Générale de Surveillance SA* v. *Islamic Republic of Pakistan*, ICSID Case No. ARB/01/13, Decision of the Tribunal on Objections to Jurisdiction, 6 August 2003.

[119] *SGS Société Générale de Surveillance SA* v. *Republic of the Philippines*, ICSID Case No. ARB/02/6, Decision of the Tribunal on Objections to Jurisdiction, 29 January 2004.

que le TBI prévoit le recours à ce même mécanisme, l'investisseur peut demander l'établissement de deux tribunaux CIRDI différents car les deux litiges ne sont pas les mêmes."[120]

The second main reason why contract and treaty claims may lead to parallel proceedings is the lack of a rule of exhaustion of local remedies in investment arbitration, unlike in general international law. In general international law – and under the system of diplomatic protection that preceded the investment treaty era – the exhaustion of local remedies is and was the default rule for a claimant to gain access to international law remedies and tribunals. In investment arbitration, the default rule is reversed: the general rule is that there is no requirement to exhaust local remedies unless express provision is made for that, for example in the treaty.

For instance, Article 26 of the ICSID Convention provides that consent to arbitration is "to the exclusion of any other remedy", including local remedies. A State "may require the exhaustion of local . . . remedies" as a condition of "consent to arbitration". Only Guatemala has notified ICSID that it will require the exhaustion of local remedies as a condition for consent to arbitration under ICSID.

The exhaustion of local remedies rule would minimise the risk of parallel proceedings as it would ensure that there would only be one ongoing set of proceedings in relation to the same dispute at any given point in time. However, this rule could increase the length and costs of proceedings, as investors would have to complete domestic litigation before invoking investment arbitration.

In summary, the combination of these two factors increases the risk of parallel proceedings in investment arbitration. Contracts and treaties are not just different

---

[120] Ben Hamida, note 110, at pp. 568-569.

sources of legal rights – rooted in national and international law, respectively. They are also sources of different legal fora to adjudicate disputes arising thereunder. The lack of a rule of exhaustion of local remedies in investment law further exacerbates the issue. Investors can file investment claims without resorting to local remedies, even where the contract contains an exclusive domestic forum selection clause. Parallel claims are thus likely to arise.

2. *The problem of vertical claims*

The *Lauder/CME* v. *Czech Republic* case is an example of vertical claims. Mr Lauder owned 99 per cent of CME's shares, and brought claims arising from the same investment chain: from the main investment company and its near sole shareholder. Vertical claims are brought by investors who are linked by a chain of corporate ownership, such as the parent company, the subsidiary, the parent company's shareholders, and so on. This ownership structure can range from simple to complex.

To illustrate, consider the following scenario: D has a contract with State X, but State X takes actions that breach D's contract rights and diminish the value of the share of D's direct and indirect shareholders, a loss of volume known as "reflective loss". Can A, B, C, E and F have a cause of action against State X? This issue has been extensively analysed by the Organisation for Economic Co-operation and Development (OECD), leading to the publication of several working papers [121]. Let us examine

---

[121] D. Gaukrodger, "Investment Treaties as Corporate Law: Shareholder Claims and Issues of Consistency", OECD Working Papers on International Investment, 2013, 2013/03, http://dx.doi.org/10.1787/5k3w9t44mt0v-en; D. Gaukrodger, "Investment Treaties and Shareholder Claims for Reflective Loss: Insights from Advanced Systems of Corporate Law", OECD Working Papers on

the answers to this question under both domestic and international law before turning to investment arbitration law.

Under domestic law

The OECD notes that

"[a]dvanced systems of domestic corporate law generally apply a 'no reflective loss' principle to shareholder claims. Shareholder claims are permitted for direct injury to shareholder rights (such as voting rights). But shareholders generally cannot bring claims for reflective loss incurred as a result of injury to 'their' company (such as loss in value of shares). Only the directly-injured company can claim"[122].

Thus, the answer to our question under most systems of domestic law will be "No". Direct and indirect shareholders cannot bring claims for reflective losses – indirect losses resulting from damage to the company. They are called "reflective" losses because they merely

---

International Investment, 2014, 2014/02, http://dx.doi.org/10.1787/5jz0xvgngmr3-en; D. Gaukrodger, "Investment Treaties and Shareholder Claims: Analysis of Treaty Practice", OECD Working Papers on International Investment, 2014, 2014/03, http://dx.doi.org/10.1787/5jxvk6shpvs4-en; OECD, "The Impact of Investment Treaties on Companies, Shareholders and Creditors", in *OECD Business and Finance Outlook 2016*, 2016, http://oe.cd/1Zv, at chap. 8; OECD, Treaty Shopping and Tools for Reform, Investment Treaty Conference materials, 2018, pp. 11-15, figs. 1-3, http://oe.cd/TS-analysis; UNCITRAL, "Possible Reform of Investor-State Dispute Settlement (ISDS): Shareholder Claims and Reflective Loss – Note by the Secretariat", A/CN.9/WG.III/WP.170, 9 August 2019, https://undocs.org/en/A/CN.9/WG.III/WP.170; J. Arato *et al.*, "Reforming Shareholder Claims in ISDS", Academic Forum on ISDS Working Paper, 2019, 2019/9, http://bit.ly/ISDS_AF_SRL_2019. All links last consulted on 19 July 2022.

[122] Gaukrodger, "Analysis of Treaty Practice", *ibid.*, at p. 3.

"reflect" the losses sustained by the company. Therefore, the rule is: no cause of action for reflective losses.

Lukas Vanhonnaeker describes the "no reflective loss" principle as a " 'general principle of corporate law' recognized in most jurisdictions, regardless of whether they belong to the civil or common law legal tradition"[123]. This principle exists in the United Kingdom, France, Germany or the Netherlands, to cite but a few. For example, the French Cour de Cassation dismissed a claim for alleged loss because il "n'était que le corollaire de celui causé à la société, [et] n'avait aucun caractère personnel"[124].

Under customary international law

As a matter of customary international law, there is no cause of action for reflective losses. This is clear from the ICJ's landmark decision of 1970 in *Barcelona Traction*. In this case, Barcelona Traction, Light and Power Company Limited was a Canadian company incorporated in Toronto with subsidiaries in Spain that held concessions to develop, produce and distribute electric power in Catalonia, Spain. The controlling shareholders of Barcelona Traction were Belgian shareholders. Spain's government took actions against the Canadian company, which allegedly caused damage

---

[123] L. Vanhonnaeker, "Shareholders' Claims for Reflective Loss in Domestic Regimes, Customary International Law of Diplomatic Protection, and Human Rights Law", in *id.*, *Shareholders' Claims for Reflective Loss in International Investment Law*, Cambridge, Cambridge University Press, pp. 54-92.

[124] C. Cass Com., No. 97-20886, 15 January 2002. In England & Wales, see *Prudential Assurance Co Ltd.* v. *Newman Industries Ltd (No.2)* [1982] 1 Ch 204; *Johnson*, note 86; but see the recent Supreme Court Judgment in *Sevilleja* v. *Marex Financial Ltd.* [2020] UKSC 31, clarifying and substantially confining the scope of the doctrine of reflective loss.

to the Belgian shareholders. In short, the Belgian shareholders claimed they had suffered reflective loss.

Belgium brought a claim against Spain before the ICJ under the doctrine of diplomatic protection, "seeking reparation for damage" that Spain allegedly caused to the Belgian shareholders of Barcelona Traction. In other words, it was a classic diplomatic protection claim but one based on reflective loss. The ICJ dismissed the claims, holding that shareholder claims for reflective losses for damage caused to the company are not allowed as a matter of customary international law. The ICJ stated (at para. 44 of the Judgment):

> "Notwithstanding the separate corporate personality, a wrong done to the company frequently causes prejudice to its shareholders. But the mere fact that damage is sustained by both company and shareholder does not imply that both are entitled to claim compensation. Thus no legal conclusion can be drawn from the fact that the same event caused damage simultaneously affecting several natural or juristic persons . . . In such cases, no doubt, the interests of the aggrieved are affected, but not their rights. Thus whenever a shareholder's interests are harmed by an act done to the company, it is to the latter that he must look to institute appropriate action; for although two separate entities may have suffered from the same wrong, it is only one entity whose rights have been infringed." [125]

Under current investment treaty jurisprudence

On this point, as noted by the OECD, investment treaty law allows claims from both direct and indirect shareholders, which sets it apart from both domestic law

---

[125] *Barcelona Traction, Light and Power Company, Limited,* Judgment, *ICJ Reports*, p. 3, at para. 44 (emphasis added).

and general customary international law. This means that in the scenario mentioned above, not only D but also A, B, C, E and F can initiate proceedings against State X. What was one set of proceedings under domestic and customary international law could become six under investment treaty law based on a simple corporate ownership structure, making it one of the central sources of parallel proceedings in investment arbitration.

The departure of investment arbitration law from other legal systems can be traced back to the ICSID Tribunal's decision on jurisdiction in *CMS* v. *Argentina* in 2003, which the OECD considers a "key moment" in investment treaty law. The Tribunal dismissed Argentina's objection to a claim by a minority shareholder, holding (in a part of the decision which was left intact by an *ad hoc* Annulment Committee) that CMS was a covered "investor" under the relevant BIT as the definition of "investment" therein covered – as is often the case in BITs – "shares or stock or other interests in a company", and that even minority shareholders had a direct right of action, not just under the terms of the BIT but as a "general rule" of investment law. The Tribunal stated the following:

> "The Tribunal . . . finds no bar in current international law to the concept of allowing claims by shareholders independently from those of the corporation concerned, not even if those shareholders are minority or non-controlling shareholders. Although it is true . . . that this is mostly the result of *lex specialis* and specific treaty arrangements that have so allowed, the fact is that *lex specialis* in this respect is so prevalent that it can now be considered the general rule, certainty in respect of foreign investments and increasingly in respect of other matters."[126]

---

[126] *CMS Gas Transmission Company* v. *The Republic of Argentina*, ICSID Case No. ARB/01/8, Decision of the Tribunal on Objections to Jurisdiction, 17 July 2003, para. 48.

This decision was the first to unambiguously establish that minority shareholders can claim reflective losses arising from damage caused to the underlying company.

The departure of investment tribunals from other legal systems in this area has been a recurring source of criticism against the current system of ISDS. The OECD papers have noted that this approach ignores basic notions of corporate law, including insolvency law[127], and places domestic investors in a company in an entirely different position than foreign investors in a way, which is difficult to reconcile with basic corporate law principles[128]. As a result, there have been calls to address the issue of vertical claims, most notably by Professor Gaillard at an Institut pour l'Arbitrage International conference held in Paris on 22 November 2013[129], and a number of solutions have been proposed and considered by tribunals.

A first approach: appropriate treaty-drafting?

In *Kappes* et al v. *Guatemala*, the claimants brought an arbitration claim against Guatemala under the Dominican Republic-Central America Free Trade Agreement or DR-CAFTA[130]. They were direct and indirect shareholders in Exmingua, a Guatemalan company, and filed the claims in their own names as shareholders, seeking compensation for reflective loss. DR-CAFTA includes

---

[127] D. Gaukrodger, "Claims for Reflective Loss under Investment Treaties", in OECD-Hosted Side Meeting, UNCITRAL Working Group III on ISDS Reform, Resumed 38th Session, 20-24 January 2020, Vienna, 22 January 2020, https://uncitral.un.org/sites/uncitral.un.org/files/oecd_reflective_loss_claims.pdf, at p. 14.

[128] *Ibid.*, at p. 12.

[129] The colloquium was entitled "Concurrent Proceedings : Investment Disputes: Treaty Arbitrations Brought by Shar holders".

[130] *Daniel W. Kappes and Kappes, Cassiday & Associate: Republic of Guatemala*, ICSID Case No. ARB/18/43.

specific provisions modelled after Articles 11-16 and 11-17 of the old NAFTA, which had been interpreted by the State Parties to NAFTA and by Tribunals (for example, in *Clayton* v. *Canada*) as precluding claims for reflective loss. Article 10.16.1 of DR-CAFTA reads as follows:

"1. In the event that a disputing party considers that an investment dispute cannot be settled by consultation and negotiation:

(a) the claimant, on its own behalf, may submit to arbitration under this Section a claim

    (i) that the respondent has breached

        (A) an obligation under Section A,
        (B) an investment authorization, or
        (C) an investment agreement;

    (ii) that the claimant has incurred loss or damage by reason of, or arising out of, that breach; and

(b) the claimant, on behalf of an enterprise of the respondent that is a juridical person that the claimant owns or controls directly or indirectly, may submit to arbitration under this Section a claim

    (i) that the respondent has breached

        (A) an obligation under Section A,
        (B) an investment authorization, or
        (C) an investment agreement; and

    (ii) that the enterprise has incurred loss or damage by reason of, or arising out of, that breach." (Emphasis added)

le 10.18, titled "Conditions and Limitations on of Each Party", provides:

To claim may be submitted to arbitration under ion if more than three years have elapsed late on which the claimant first acquired, or should have first acquired, knowledge of the breach alleged under Article 10.16.1 and knowledge that the claimant (for claims brought under Art. 10.16.1 *(a)*) or the enterprise (for claims brought under Art. 10.16.1 *(b)*) has incurred loss or damage.

In other words, if the controlling shareholder brings a claim under Article 10.16.1 *(b)* on behalf of its company, then it has to provide a waiver both for itself and the company (Art. 10.18.1 *(b) (ii)*).

If a claim is brought on behalf of the company pursuant to Article 10.16.1 *(b)*, then Article 10.26.2 *(b)* directs that any damages awarded must be paid to the company and not the controlling shareholder and the company would have previously waived the pursuit if any other remedy in respect of the same prejudice."

Professor Douglas held, in a dissenting opinion, that this regime achieved the same result as NAFTA and precluded claims for reflective loss[131]. In his view, the company, not its shareholders, should sue for losses suffered by the company. The majority (Kalicki, Townsend) disagreed with this position[132]. The disagreement between the majority and the dissenting opinion highlights the need for treaty-drafting solutions to be airtight if they are to effectively bar claims by shareholders for reflective loss.

A second approach: tribunal-driven rather than treaty-driven solutions

The relevant case is *Orascom* v. *Algeria*, in which Algeria took measures against a company called Djezzy for allegedly violating Algerian law. The dispute involved

---

[131] *Ibid.*, Partial Dissenting Opinion of Zachary Douglas, 13 March 2020.

[132] *Ibid.*, Decision on the Respondent's Preliminary Objection, 13 March 2020.

the following vertical corporate chain Orascom owned Weather Investments, which owned OTH which owned Djezzy. Each company had a potential claim against Algeria for measures taken against Djezzy. Specifically, Djezzy could have brought a claim under the investment contract with Algeria, OTH under its Algeria-Egypt BIT, Weather Investments under the Algeria-Italy BIT and Orascom under the Algeria-BLEU (Belgium & Luxembourg) BIT.

In practice, OTH sent a notice of dispute to Algeria under the Algeria-Egypt BIT in 2010 and initiated a Permanent Court of Arbitration (PCA) arbitration in 2012 under the same BIT, which was settled by consent award in 2015. Weather Investments also sent a notice of dispute in 2010 (less than a week after OTH) under the Algeria-Italy BIT, though it did not pursue the matter further. Orascom, at the top of the corporate chain, began ICSID proceedings against Algeria under the Algeria-BLEU BIT in 2012, which continued despite the settlement in the OTH arbitration.

In a ground-breaking decision, the tribunal dismissed Orascom's claims as inadmissible, stating that pursuing claims "at different levels of the vertical corporate chain" amounted to an "abuse of the system of investment protection"[133]. The decision has potentially significant implications, which will be discussed further in Chapter V.

3. *One measure, multiple disputes*

The most significant source of parallel proceedings in numerical terms is undoubtedly the third one, where a single State measure can impact a group or class of investors, generating multiple disputes against the State.

---

[133] *Orascom TMT Investments Sàrl* v. *People's Democratic Republic of Algeria*, ICSID Case No. ARB/12/35, Final Award, 31 May 2017, para. 545.

Unlike vertical claims, affected investors in this scenario are not linked by a chain of ownership, at least not necessarily so. However, these two sources of parallel proceedings can overlap, where a single State measure affects both independent investors and vertically-linked investors simultaneously. For now, we focus on independent investors alone.

This source of parallel proceedings results from three factors. First, State measures typically affect not only one entity but a whole group or class of entities. This is no different in the field of foreign investment, where State measures can impact a whole group or class of foreign investors as well. Second, investment treaties typically feature open-ended arbitration offers. This means that all foreign investors who may potentially be affected by a State measure can bring claims against the State, even if there is no privity of contract between the investor and the State. Finally, there is no system of binding precedent in international arbitration, nor could there be given the *ad hoc* nature of each tribunal constituted to hear each dispute. As a result, the outcomes of previous cases can only have persuasive authority on later cases, which gives investors an incentive to pursue claims even if the previous outcomes were not favourable.

The combination of these factors has led to a series of so-called "waves" of investment arbitrations against States. As noted earlier, Argentina was the first to experience a major wave of investment claims due to measures it enacted following the 2001 financial crisis. To date, Argentina remains the host State with the highest number of investment arbitrations brought against it. Other States that have been on the receiving end of "waves" of claims include Spain, Italy, the Czech Republic, Venezuela, Egypt and Ecuador.

In numerical terms, there is a significant difference between vertical claims and disputes involving multiple claimants with no ownership or other link, which we might refer to as "multi-claimant disputes". Vertical claims usually result in at most a few separate proceedings. In the *Orascom* case, up to four separate proceedings could have been brought against Algeria, but only two were actually brought, with a notice of dispute filed in a third. In contrast, multi- claimant disputes can affect hundreds, even thousands of potential investors. For instance, in the largest multi-claimant dispute scenario so far, 195,000 independent claimants filed a single investment arbitration against Argentina (*Beccara* v. *Argentina*, later *Abaclat* v. *Argentina*). Therefore, this source of parallel proceedings can lead to an exponentially higher number of disputes than the vertical claims scenario.

In *Orascom*, all four potential claimants in the vertical corporate chain could have viably brought claims against Algeria. This was possible as they had the means to do so and were essentially in the same ownership. However, this was probably not the case in the *Beccara* arbitration, where the bringing of a single claim was probably an economic imperative to make the proceedings viable for the claimants.

When it comes to terminology, we must exercise caution since the phenomenon of multiple disputes arising from the same State measure has led to new terms in this field. The term "mass claims" implies that the State measure affects a large number of potential claimants, as was the case in *Abaclat*[134]. However, this need not be the case, and a State measure could impact only a few independent and unaffiliated foreign investors, such as oil companies. Nonetheless, the term "mass claims" is not misleading and can be used, as it commonly is.

On the other hand, the term "class action" can be misleading because it has a precise technical meaning under US law – as the tribunal in *Ambiente Ufficio* v.

---

[134] *Abaclat and Others* v. *Argentine Republic*, ICSID Case No. ARB/07/5.

reveals several key points. First, the system appears to favour investors in some respects, as they often have multiple opportunities to succeed in claims against host States over essentially the same dispute. However, States may also seek to initiate parallel proceedings as a defensive tactic to make the investors' claims financially unviable. Second, investment arbitration has the potential to generate more undesirable parallel proceedings than any of the other type of interaction examined in this course, that is court v. tribunal and commercial arbitrations with no investment arbitration element. Conversely, parallel proceedings may also be seen as undesirable in the sense that they can render claims financially unviable, leaving investors with no legal recourse. Finally, investment arbitration presents the greatest challenges with respect to undesirable parallel proceedings, making it an area with the greatest room for improvement. Chapter V will therefore focus on identifying solutions that are tailored to this particular field.

CHAPTER V

WHERE TO FROM HERE?
THE SEARCH FOR PRACTICAL SOLUTIONS

Before we delve into the goals of the final chapter, let us briefly take stock of the ground that we have traversed. In Chapter I, we defined the subject matter and established criteria to distinguish acceptable from undesirable parallel proceedings. In Chapters II to IV, we conducted a theoretical analysis of potential conflicts, overlaps, and friction among adjudicating bodies charged with deciding international disputes. Specifically, we looked at three areas of interaction:

(a) *National courts* v. *international arbitral tribunals*
(b) *International arbitral tribunal* v. *international arbitral tribunal* in a commercial setting with no investment arbitration element
(c) *International arbitral tribunal* v. *international arbitral tribunal* with an investment arbitration element

In this final chapter, we aim to use our analysis to propose new solutions to the problem of undesirable parallel proceedings that have no place in a well-functioning system for settling international disputes. Substantial doctrinal and scholarly efforts were made in 2006 to address parallel proceedings, notably the ILA "Recommendations on *Lis Pendens* and *Res Judicata* and Arbitration" and the Geneva Colloquium on Consolidation of Proceedings in Investment Arbitration. These have provided a useful analytical framework and a basis to act for tribunals seeking to actively manage such issues. But, as we have seen, these seminal studies have had a limited aspect in practice, while the development of investment arbitration has exacerbated the scale, of the problem and nature.

Therefore, in this chapter, we will discuss separately potential solutions for each of the three fields covered in Chapters II to IV, namely interaction with national courts, interaction in the field of commercial arbitration, and interaction in the field of investment arbitration.

A. *National courts*

We have seen that most interactions with national courts involve the principle of competence-competence. However, there seems to be little appetite among States to adopt negative competence-competence, which would limit the scope for interaction between courts and tribunals by giving preference (priority in time) to tribunals. I would for my part encourage developing States, where the judiciary may not yet be fully familiar with the principles of international arbitration and their implementation, to consider adopting negative competence-competence, as Mauritius has done.

Most undesirable interactions between courts and tribunals occur due to national courts erroneously taking jurisdiction in cases where there is an agreement to arbitrate between the parties. In response, other courts, usually the courts of the seat, may take action to protect the agreement, sometimes through anti-suit relief. The tribunal may also be tempted to protect its own jurisdiction through such relief, leading to contentious exchanges of prohibitory injunctions between courts and tribunals. To avoid this, developing States could adopt a simple and mechanical rule requiring them to decline jurisdiction whenever an agreement to arbitrate *prima facie* exists. This approach, as seen in the Mauritian International Arbitration Act, would minimise the points of contact between the arbitral process and national courts and be in line with the spirit of the New York Convention, which has been ratified by over 160 States. The Mauritian Act was specifically designed for this purpose, with the assistance of UNCITRAL, and could serve as a model for other developing jurisdictions.

In addition to adopting negative competence-competence, the Mauritian Act has other features that could minimise the points of contact between the arbitral process and national courts. For example, all international arbitration matters (including the consideration of stays of jurisdiction in favour of arbitration) are assigned to a panel of three Designated Judges with specific knomledge of arbitration by way of Section 42 of the Act. These judges, selected from a pool of six, receive special training in international arbitration, such as the courses of the Arbitration Academy in Paris, and develop their expertise further by consistently hearing and determining arbitration applications. This approach has also been adopted in developed jurisdictions, such as France, where an International Chamber of the Paris Court of Appeals has been established specifically to handle arbitral matters. Such specialised bodies can help ensure consistent and expert handling of international arbitration matters, reducing the potential for friction between courts and tribunals.

B. *Commercial arbitration*

In the field of commercial arbitration, how can the limitations of the *res judicata* and *lis pendens* doctrines, and of consolidation and joinder be improved? There have been promising developments in the area of consolidation and joinder in recent years, with many arbitral institutions introducing rules to allow for these procedures. The Singapore International Arbitration Centre ("SIAC") has in addition proposed a protocol to allow consolidation even when proceedings arise under different institutional rules. We will explore these developments, before considering whether further action could be taken at the higher level of national legislation.

1. *Evolution of institutional rules*

Starting with the evolution of institutional rules on consolidation and consent, this discussion will focus on the ICC and LCIA rules, with the understanding that other institutions have made similar changes and are likely to continue doing so.

The ICC Rules have seen significant evolution in consolidation provisions over the past twenty-five years through four versions of the rules, which came into effect in 1998, 2012, 2017 and 2021. The 1998 version contained the following skeletal provision in Article 4 (6):

> "When a party submits a Request in connection with a legal relationship in respect of which arbitration proceedings between the same parties are already pending under these Rules, the Court may, at the request of a party, decide to include the claims contained in the Request in the pending proceedings provided that the Terms of Reference have not been signed or approved by the Court. Once the Terms of Reference have been signed or approved by the Court, claims may only be included in the pending proceedings subject to the provisions of Article 19."

This provision was limited and very narrow, applying to the same "legal relationship" between "the same parties". If these two requirements were met, the "claims" in the second arbitration could be added to the arbitration already pending. This was *not* a consolidation or joinder provision but simply allowed new claims to be added to an existing arbitration.

The 2012 version of the ICC Rules marked a significant step forward, providing a broader and more detailed framework for consolidation. Article 10 of the 2012 version provided as follows:

> "The Court may, at the request of a party, consolidate two or more arbitrations pending under the Rules into a single arbitration, where:
>
> *(a)* the parties have agreed to consolidation; or
> *(b)* all of the claims in the arbitrations are made under the same arbitration agreement; or
> *(c)* where the claims in the arbitrations are made under more than one arbitration agreement, the arbitrations are between the same parties, the disputes in the arbitrations arise in connection with the same legal relationship, and the Court finds the arbitration agreements to be compatible.
>
> In deciding whether to consolidate, the Court may take into account any circumstances it considers to be relevant including whether one or more arbitrators have been confirmed or appointed in more than one of the arbitrations and, if so, whether the same or different persons have been confirmed or appointed.
>
> When arbitrations are consolidated, they shall be consolidated into the arbitration that commenced first, unless otherwise agreed by all parties."

Unlike the 1998 version, the 2012 version explicitly refers to "consolidation" and "arbitrations" and not merely to "claims", and does not contain time limits for consolidation requests (i.e. it is not limited to the period when the request for arbitration is filed). Moreover, the 2012 version identifies and systematises three possible routes to consolidation: *(a)* with the agreement of all parties; *(b)* all claims are made under the same arbitration agreement; and *(c)* the claims made are under different arbitration agreements. In this last route, the parties and legal relationship must be the same and the arbitration agreements must be compatible.

As the timeline shows, these changes were made after the work done in 2006 by the ILA and the Geneva Colloquium. The ICC's consolidation rules remained unchanged in the third version, issued in 2017. The latest update, in 2021, introduces relatively minor changes to the 2012/2017 version. The new Article 10 reads thus:

"The Court may, at the request of a party, consolidate two or more arbitrations pending under the Rules into a single arbitration, where:

(a) the parties have agreed to consolidation; or
(b) all of the claims in the arbitrations are made under the same arbitration agreement or agreements; or
(c) the claims in the arbitrations are not made under the same arbitration agreement or agreements, but the arbitrations are between the same parties, the disputes in the arbitrations arise in connection with the same legal relationship, and the Court finds the arbitration agreements to be compatible.

In deciding whether to consolidate, the Court may take into account any circumstances it considers to be relevant, including whether one or more arbitrators have been confirmed or appointed in more than one of the arbitrations and, if so, whether the same or different persons have been confirmed or appointed.

When arbitrations are consolidated, they shall be consolidated into the arbitration that commenced first, unless otherwise agreed by all parties."

What has changed is the wording of scenario *(c)*, that is, consolidation of arbitrations other than "under the same arbitration agreement" (scenario *b*). In the 2012/2017 version, scenario *(c)* applied where the claims were made "under more than one arbitration agreement", whereas in the 2021 version this scenario applies when the claims "are not made under the same arbitration agreement or agreements". This draws a clearer limit between scenarios *(b)* and *(c)*: scenario *(b)* covers arbitrations based on "the same arbitration agreement", whereas scenario *(c)* covers the rest: arbitrations "not" based on the "same arbitration agreement". This makes more logical sense as two arbitration agreements could conceptually be "the same" and "more than one" simultaneously if they are included in separate contracts, making it difficult to ascertain what scenario would apply under the circumstances.

How could the ICC rules be further improved? There could be further guidelines on what makes two arbitration clauses "compatible". For example, different seats, languages, numbers of arbitrators and versions of the rules could be taken into account. Additionally, the ICC Court could have the power, on an opt-out basis, to change one or more of the arbitration clauses to enable consolidation where necessary, such as changing the seat, number of arbitrators or language. For example, if one arbitration is seated in Paris and the other in Amsterdam, the ICC Court could decide to consolidate the case in either Paris or Amsterdam depending on multiple factors, such as which one was brought first, what is the main dispute, which of the two would be more neutral and efficient, and so on. This could not be objected to on the basis of consent or party autonomy, as parties would be subscribing to this regime *ex ante* when agreeing to the ICC Rules in their contract without opting out thereof.

The new 2021 Expedited Procedure Rules already allow the ICC Court to appoint a sole arbitrator regardless of what the arbitration clause says, providing a precedent for such a regime. Appendix VI, Article 2 of the Expedited Procedure Rules provide that "the Court may, notwithstanding any contrary provision of the arbitration agreement, appoint a sole arbitrator". If the ICC Court can amend the arbitration agreement for the sake of efficiency, why should it not have the power to do so even where higher-ranking values than efficiency are at stake, such as avoiding contradictory decisions and erosion of confidence in the system? The number of arbitrators, language and seat could be amended for consolidation, with a caveat that the ICC Court should ensure that this does not result in manifest unfairness or injustice in the circumstances of the case.

The LCIA Arbitration Rules have undergone changes over time, similar to those seen in the ICC Rules. Three versions of the rules have been applicable during the same period: the 1998, 2014 and 2020 versions.

The 1998 version of the rules did not include any provisions on consolidation. However, it did allow for joinder under Article 22 (1) *(h)*, which authorised the arbitral tribunal

> "to allow, only upon the application of a party, one or more third persons to be joined in the arbitration as a party provided any such third person and the applicant party have consented thereto in writing, and thereafter to make a single final award, or separate awards, in respect of all parties so implicated in the arbitration".

Joinder could therefore be ordered by the tribunal against the will of the non-applying party, but it required the consent of the third party that was to be joined.

The 2014 version of the LCIA Rules marked a significant improvement, similar to the 2012 ICC Rules. The arbitral tribunal and the LCIA Court were recognised as having the power to consolidate two or more arbitrations under certain circumstances. Additionally, the joinder provision in Article 22 was amended thus:

> "22.1 The Arbitral Tribunal shall have the power, upon the application of any party or…upon its own initiative, but in either case only after giving the parties a reasonable opportunity to state their views and upon such terms (as to costs and otherwise) as the Arbitral Tribunal may decide:
>
> . . .

(viii) to allow one or more third persons to be joined in the arbitration as a party provided any such third person and the applicant party have consented to such joinder in writing following the Commencement Date or (if earlier) in the Arbitration Agreement; and thereafter to make a single final award, or separate awards, in respect of all parties so implicated in the arbitration;

(ix) to order, with the approval of the LCIA Court, the consolidation of the arbitration with one or more other arbitrations into a single arbitration subject to the LCIA Rules where all the parties to the arbitrations to be consolidated so agree in writing;

(x) to order, with the approval of the LCIA Court, the consolidation of the arbitration with one or more other arbitrations subject to the LCIA Rules commenced under the same arbitration agreement or any compatible arbitration agreement(s) between the same disputing parties, provided that no arbitral tribunal has yet been formed by the LCIA Court for such other arbitration(s) or, if already formed, that such tribunal(s) is(are) composed of the same arbitrators;

. . .

22.6 Without prejudice to the generality of Articles 22.1 *(ix)* and *(x)*, the LCIA Court may determine, after giving the parties a reasonable opportunity to state their views, that two or more arbitrations, subject to the LCIA Rules and commenced under the same arbitration agreement between the same disputing parties, shall be consolidated to form one single arbitration subject to the LCIA Rules, provided that no arbitral tribunal has yet been formed by the LCIA Court for any of the arbitrations to be consolidated."

Article 22.1 *(ix)* thus mirrors Article 10 *(a)* of the ICC Rules, and 22.1 *(x)* mirrors Articles 10 *(b)* and *(c)*, encompassing two scenarios in the same provision: consolidation based on the "same arbitration" agreement and consolidation based on a "compatible" arbitration agreement.

The 2020 version of the LCIA Rules went further, featuring a separate provision solely dedicated to consolidation and concurrent proceedings:

> "Article 22A Power to Order Consolidation/Concurrent Conduct of Arbitrations
>
> 22.7 The Arbitral Tribunal shall have the power to order with the approval of the LCIA Court, upon the application of any party, after giving all affected parties a reasonable opportunity to state their views and upon such terms (as to costs and otherwise) as the Arbitral Tribunal may decide:
>
> *(i)* the consolidation of the arbitration with one or more other arbitrations into a single arbitration subject to the LCIA Rules where all the parties to the arbitrations to be consolidated so agree in writing;
>
> *(ii)* the consolidation of the arbitration with one or more other arbitrations subject to the LCIA Rules and commenced under the same arbitration agreement or any compatible arbitration agreement(s) and either between the same disputing parties or arising out of the same transaction or series of related transactions, provided that no arbitral tribunal has yet been formed by the LCIA Court for such other arbitration(s) or, if already formed, that such arbitral tribunal(s) is(are) composed of the same arbitrators; and

> *(iii)* that two or more arbitrations, subject to the LCIA Rules and commenced under the same arbitration agreement or any compatible arbitration agreement(s) and either between the same disputing parties or arising out of the same transaction or series of related transactions, shall be conducted concurrently where the same arbitral tribunal is constituted in respect of each arbitration.
>
> 22.8 Without prejudice to the generality of Article 22.7, the LCIA Court may:
>
> *(i)* consolidate an arbitration with one or more other arbitrations into a single arbitration subject to the LCIA Rules where all the parties to the arbitrations to be consolidated so agree in writing; and
>
> *(ii)* determine, after giving the parties a reasonable opportunity to state their views, that two or more arbitrations, subject to the LCIA Rules and commenced under the same arbitration agreement or any compatible arbitration agreement(s) and either between the same disputing parties or arising out of the same transaction or series of related transactions, shall be consolidated to form one single arbitration subject to the LCIA Rules, provided that no arbitral tribunal has yet been formed by the LCIA Court for any of the arbitrations to be consolidated."

The 2020 LCIA Rules thus introduce an important development: consolidation can be ordered not just between "the same disputing parties" but also when the arbitrations arise out "of the same transaction or series of related transaction", therefore significantly expanding the scope of possible consolidation.

Article 22.7 *(iii)* also proposes a solution absent from any version of the ICC Rules or in any previous version of the LCIA Rules: the possibility that the same tribunal may hear two or more arbitrations concurrently: this will usually mean the same procedural calendar for written submissions and hearings in the arbitrations, but two separate awards. The procedure is coordinated but the arbitrations remain legally distinct.

It is likely that future versions of arbitration rules worldwide will adopt the approach taken by the latest editions of the ICC and LCIA rules. This trend represents a positive development, as it enables the inclusion of specific provisions regarding consolidation of arbitrations within the institutional framework, which records the parties' *ex ante* consent to consolidation one level up from the specific arbitration clause in their contract, thus opening the door to the possibility of consolidating disputes submitted to the same institution. To be bound by this *ex ante* consent to consolidation, the parties need not be parties to the same arbitration clauses; it suffices that they have agreed in some form or another, and that could be in different contracts, to the application of the relevant institutional rules.

However, this solution has its limitations, especially in cases where disputes involve arbitration clauses that refer to different institutions, such as ICC and LCIA, or LCIA and SIAC. In such situations, there is a risk of legal uncertainty, as each institution may seek to consolidate disputes under its own rules, which may result in turf wars similar to those that arose between the ICC and SIAC after the Singapore Court of Appeal's 2009 decision in *Insigma* v. *Alstom*, which validated a hybrid clause that provided for arbitration under the ICC Rules but was managed by SIAC rather than the ICC Court[146].

---

[146] *Insigma Technology Co Ltd.* v. *Alstom Technology Ltd.*, [2009] SGCA 24.

2. *SIAC Consolidation Protocol*

What can be done to deal with such situations? SIAC has proposed a creative solution to the problem in the form of a cross-institution Consolidation Protocol designed to address it. Although it has not yet been implemented, it is still being promoted and as a welcome and worthy effort to design a system capable of consolidating related disputes arising under different arbitration rules.

The Consolidation Protocol identifies the nature of the problem and the benefits of the protocol thus:

> "5. The lack of any existing mechanism for "cross-institution" consolidation of arbitrations subject to different institutional arbitration rules substantially limits the types of disputes that can be consolidated. In many cases, related contracts in a single project or set of transactions will contain agreements to arbitrate under different institutional arbitration rules (e.g., SIAC and ICC) – which, as already noted, cannot be consolidated together. In turn, this prevents related disputes, which otherwise meet the criteria for consolidation, from being heard together and thus limits the ability of arbitration as a dispute resolution mechanism from serving the needs of users. Although there is very limited statistical data on how frequently related disputes arise under different institutional rules, anecdotal evidence suggests that this is not an uncommon occurrence. This is unsurprising given the increasingly complex nature of contemporary business transactions.
>
> 6. This shortcoming in the existing treatment of consolidation by arbitral institutions can be remedied through institutional cooperation. In particular, as discussed below, the efficiency and efficacy of the international arbitral process would be materially improved by the adoption of a consolidation protocol by leading arbitral institutions, providing for the

cross-institution consolidation of arbitrations, where such proceedings otherwise satisfy the criteria for consolidation."

The Consolidation Protocols sets a basic framework to answer two key questions in the event of consolidation in a cross-institution scenario. The first question is *who* decides whether to consolidate two arbitrations subject to different arbitration rules. The Protocol considers two options: a joint committee of the institutions involved or just one of the institutions – to be selected according to objective criteria. The best option, according to the Protocol, is for a joint committee to decide the question of consolidation based on joint criteria:

> "[A]rbitral institutions could adopt a consolidation protocol that sets out a new, standalone mechanism for addressing the timing of consolidation applications, the appropriate decision-maker (i.e. the institution(s) or the tribunal) and the applicable criteria to determine when arbitral proceedings are sufficiently related to warrant cross-institution consolidation. A joint committee appointed from members of the Courts or Boards of the concerned arbitral institutions would be mandated to decide the applications, with a specific committee being appointed for each application.
>
> [B]oth institutions play a role in deciding whether the standards for consolidation have been met and whether the proceedings should be consolidated. New consolidation rules will also avoid the need for either institution to interpret the rules of the other. From a process perspective, it is unlikely to be arduous for the institutions to reach agreement on a consolidation protocol given the relatively limited number of issues that arise in relation to consolidation."

The Consolidation Protocol also flags five "key issues" that it must address, including the identity of a decision-maker for decisions regarding consolidation, standards for consolidation of arbitrations, timing of the application and status of existing tribunal appointments, partial consolidation, and reasons for consolidation decisions.

The second question is *who* administers the consolidated case once the decision to consolidate has been made. Here again, there are two options: the new consolidated arbitration will be either "jointly administered" or will be administered by "only one institution . . . under its own rules". SIAC considers that the better option, for practical purposes, is for only one institution to administer the case since it is easier and less expensive than two institutions jointly administering the case under new joint arbitral rules.

But how to choose which arbitral institution would administer the case? The Consolidation Protocol proposes objective criteria for selecting the administering institution, including the number of cases to be consolidated and the aggregate value of disputes. The Protocol considers the criteria of time, subject matter, and nationality and domicile of the parties to be "unattractive" and "unappealing".

The Consolidation Protocol is a welcome and worthy effort to design a system capable of consolidating related disputes that meet the criteria for consolidation. It proposes a framework for addressing key questions related to cross-institutional consolidation, including who decides whether to consolidate and who administers the consolidated case. By providing a solution to the problem of cross-institutional consolidation, the Protocol has the potential to improve the efficiency and efficacy of the international arbitral process.

3. *Recording* ex ante *consent within national legislation?*

Before concluding our discussion of consolidation and joinder, it is worth considering whether national court legislation can do more to facilitate these procedures. As we saw in Chapter III, the Swiss Federal Tribunal ordered the consolidation of related arbitrations in *Andersen Consulting Business* v. *Arthur Andersen Business*, despite differences in the wording and type of arbitration clauses involved, with some referring to the ICC and others being *ad hoc* (i.e. non-institutional) clauses [147].

To promote consolidation and joinder further, more States could follow the lead of New Zealand and Mauritius by empowering their national courts to order these procedures within their jurisdiction. Mauritius, for example, has provisions in its legislation (see Articles 3 and 4 of the First Schedule to the Mauritanian Act) that allow for consolidation and joinder, although they only apply if the parties have specifically opted into them. Article 3 is a lengthy provision that deals with the mechanics of consolidation, while Article 4 is a short provision empowering the court to order joinder where the party sought to be joined has agreed to in writing (which may be by way of an arbitration agreement).

However, one should not overestimate the impact of national court legislation in this regard. First, such provisions will not be effective if the proceedings being consolidated have their seats in different jurisdictions. This issue could be addressed through an inter-State protocol, perhaps part of a wider protocol annexed to the New York Convention, but this is not a realistic scenario. Second, the experience in Mauritius suggests that parties may not have much interest in opting into these provisions. Therefore, institutional rules remain the more promising avenue for facilitating consolidation and joinder, which could ideally be supplemented by some form of the SIAC Protocol in the future.

---

[147] See note 99.

4. Res judicata *and* lis pendens, *a greater role for abuse of process?*

Turning now to the way forward in commercial arbitration, we must consider whether more can be done with regard to the doctrines of *res judicata* and *lis pendens*. As we have seen, the narrow application of *res judicata*, due to the strict triple-identity test, means it will rarely be satisfied in practice. *Lis pendens*, on the other hand, could be more widely applied as a matter of discretionary case management, particularly in cases where proceedings cover related but not identical issues, similar to the regime under the Brussels Regulation.

However, the most significant recent development has been the increased role of the doctrine of abuse of process, particularly in Anglo-Saxon jurisdictions. It is a promising development, one to approach with caution, in that it operates separately from *res judicata* and issue estoppel in a way with relaxes the strictures of the triple-identity test. It protects litigants from having to defend the same issue twice, even where the parties are not identical, and debars a litigant from pursuing in fresh proceedings claims which they ought to have brought but failed to bring in previous proceedings.

We examined the example of England in Chapter III, where the Court of Appeal unequivocally confirmed the application of the doctrine to arbitral awards. However, difficulties remain. First, what of the use of the doctrine by a later tribunal, as opposed to a court? Can a tribunal refuse to adjudicate a claim submitted to it in circumstances where *res judicata* and issue estoppel do not formally apply, but it is argued that pursuing the claim would engage one of the two scenarios mentioned above (protection from repeated defence of the same issue and claims by instalment)? Second, practical difficulties exist for a later tribunal trying to access or use the findings of an earlier tribunal.

The first issue may be resolved through jurisprudential developments, as the law seems to be moving towards greater acceptance of the use of the abuse of process doctrine. The second issue could also resolved judicially given that the confidentiality of commercial arbitration and the exceptions thereto are often dealt with in case law rather than statute. This is part of a wider debate as to the continued place of confidentiality in commercial arbitration.

C. *Investment arbitration*

Finally, let's delve into investment arbitration and the possible solutions to address its challenges. Investment arbitration poses new, significant challenges related to parallel proceedings that have been persisting for almost two decades. As mentioned in Chapter IV, investment arbitration is fertile ground for parallel proceedings for several reasons, including the dual contract and treaty substratum of investment claims, the issue of vertical claims, and waves of claims stemming from the same State measure.

This issue, along with its implications for the coherence and consistency of the ISDS system, is a central symptom of the so-called "crisis of legitimacy" that has plagued ISDS for several years. This term describes the increasing lack of confidence that those outside the ISDS system, and a few inside it, have in the system. This situation has prompted concrete action, notably UNCITRAL's work in the field of transparency, which I had the privilege to chair. The following three points can be drawn from UNCITRAL's work.

First, the way in which UNCITRAL began its work in this area is instructive. The transparency project was not a topic calmly picked by the Commission for future work, but was brought to the fore forcefully by certain States, NGOs and the UN Special Representative for

Business and Human Rights, Professor John Ruggie, during UNCITRAL's work on what became the UNCITRAL Rules 2010. Consequently, the Commission had to agree to undertake immediate work in the area with a specific focus on ISDS in order to preserve the integrity of the UNCITRAL Rules as a set of universal rules applicable to both commercial and investor-State arbitration. Interestingly, many arbitration practitioners rejected the NGOs and Professor Ruggie's call for reform, most notably the Milan Club of Arbitrators' in a written submission. See UNCITRAL working Group 2's Report on the work of its 48th Session (New York, 4-8 February 2008), Doc. A/cn.9/646 at p. 21 (accessible on the UNCITRAL website).

Second, the transparency project concluded through a creative mechanism, a multilateral convention (the Mauritius Convention), which relies on the provision of Article 30 of the Vienna Convention on the Law of Treaties to effect overall procedural reform affecting all existing investment treaties. This provides a possible way forward for wider procedural reform beyond transparency.

Third, following UNCITRAL's work, the calls for wider procedural reform have become louder, and it has become increasingly clear in that forum that meaningful reform of the current, arbitration-based ISDS system is necessary. While some contend that much of the criticism levelled at the system is unfounded, two points appear difficult to ignore. First, those within the system have done little to reform the system. As a result, many States believe that sovereign States themselves, and not internal actors, should reform the system to retain its principal attributes, including neutrality [148], while addressing its

---

[148] See, in particular, G. Kaufmann-Kohler and M. Potesta, "Can the Mauritius Convention Serve as a Model for the Reform of Investor-State Arbitration in Connection with the Introduction of a Permanent Investment Tribunal or

perceived problems. Second, whether those problems are real or perceived matters little, as ISDS has become, a staple feature of mainstream news outlets such as the *New York Times*, *Le Monde*, *The Guardian* and *The London Times*, and always for the wrong reasons: so that a mechanism which was meant to despoliticise the settlement of disputes between investors and States has itself become highly politicised; and is thus now arguably hindering rather than fostering trade and investment flows, as States that would welcome such flows run scaned of the real or perceived legal sister that are now associated with them.

This clearly calls for reforms. The question is how far those should go. As UNCITRAL has been debating that question over the past three years, it has clearly emerged that the main area of concern arises from the very nature of the current – arbitration-based – system: because that system relies on the ad hoc resolution of disputes by one-off panels, fragmentation, and a resulting lack of coherence and of consistency of solutions, are hard-wired in the system. That problem is exacerbated by the attitude of some, though not all, arbitrators who still come to this field with a commercial arbitrator's mindset and thus do not see themselves as being under a duty to uphold the systemic integrity of the system. Rather, they understand their duty as being limited to resolving the particular dispute which has been brought before them by these particular parties, in line with the words of Mance LJ (as he then was) in Lincoln as to what is expected of commercial arbitrators [149].

---

an Appeal Mechanism? Analysis and Roadmap, https://papers.ssrn.com/sol3/papers.cfm?abstract_id=3455511; Kaufmann-Kohler and Potesta, "The Composition of a Multilateral Investment Court and of an Appeal Mechanism for Investment Awards", https://papers.ssrn.com/sol3/papers.cfm?abstract_id=3457310.

[149] *Lincoln National Life Insurance Co v. Sun Life Assurance Co of Canada* [2004] EWCA Civ. 1660, at para. 68 *("The*

The symptoms of that fragmentation are well known and our subject, the problem of parallel or concurrent related proceedings, is one such key symptom. Despite numerous calls for action, and some creative solutions devised inter alia by Professor Kaufmann-Koher based on abuse of process, they continue to plague the field.

Another related symptom is that while some tribunals – again and unfortunately not all tribunals – do strive to develop harmonised legal standards, the lack of any system of binding precedent, or of any mechanism to resolve conflicting authorities, continues to prevent the emergence of legal clarity – thus enhancing the risk of inconsistency arising from parallel proceedings. The examples often referred to are the interpretation of MFN clauses or of umbrella clauses. But the problem is more fundamental. For it remains the case that for every treaty standard, FET, FPS, expropriation, Counsel on both sides of the dispute feel duty-bound to take every possible point – however tenuous – on the off-chance that this particular panel of arbitrators, the writings of which have been analysed prior to appointment, will reach a solution favourable to their side. That is not an efficient system of dispute resolution. Parties in contractual proceedings before domestic courts do not spend days arguing, in every single contractual case, on what 'consideration' means if they are in England or on the notion of vice du consentement if they are in France. The meaning of these notions has long been settled by the superior courts of that country, and the debate focuses on their application to the facts of the case in light of the specific language used in the contract in question. There is similarly no reason why one could not have settled principles governing the meaning of FET or FPS, always subject of course to the specific language used in the specific treaty.

---

arbitrators in each arbitration are appointed to decide the disputes in that arbitration between the particular parties to that arbitration.").

The question is thus no longer whether the ISDS system should be reformed, but rather how and how far. For some the fact that these problems are systemic means that systemic solutions are required; and that no amount of incremental change will suffice. Others argue for a retention of the current system but with meaningful 'incremental' changes. These two ways forward are not antithetic, at least not in the short or medium term, as any systemic solution would take time to devise and implement. The path chosen by UNCITRAL has accordingly been to work in parallel both on incremental and systemic reform. The following sections will explore the possible reform options concerning or affecting parallel proceedings.

1. Incremental reform

Starting with incremental reform, which refers to changes to the existing system of arbitration-based ISDS that preserve the system, there are two notable areas to consider. In addition, as with commercial arbitration, it is worth examining whether there is potential for a wider role for the doctrine of abuse of process.

The first area of incremental reform involves the possibility of a straightforward yet potentially effective "soft law" instrument. This would come in the form of a declaration by the UN General Assembly (UNGA), similar to the interpretative declarations it made regarding the New York Convention in 2006. This could be accompanied by a "toolbox" for parties and arbitrators, providing guidance on how to apply the soft law instrument.

The second possibility is that of a cross-institution consolidation protocol, similar to the one being promoted by SIAC in the commercial arbitration field. This protocol would aim to consolidate parallel proceedings, thereby reducing the risk of inconsistent outcomes.

Soft law on parallel proceedings

The first possible tool for incremental reform would be a soft law instrument formally highlights the differences between commercial arbitration and investment arbitration and providing a "toolbox" of strategies that parties and tribunals could use to coordinate parallel proceedings and minimise the risk of inconsistencies between them.

The usefulness of such an instrument lies in how the ISDS system was created and developed. While arbitration has a long pedigree as a form of dispute settlement in the public international law arena, the fact is that investment arbitration had largely borrowed from commercial arbitration in terms of procedure and personnel. As a result, practitioners in the field, including arbitrators and counsel, often approach investment arbitration with the reflexes and instincts of a commercial practitioner: to serve the parties and resolve the dispute without any duty to the ISDS system as a whole or any other interests. This can lead to a narrow focus on the specific interests of the parties before them and a reluctance to share information or coordinate with other tribunals.

However, it is now beyond doubt that investment arbitration is fundamentally different from commercial arbitration, and arbitrators have a duty to go beyond the specific interests of the parties before them and consider the systemic implications of their decisions and the impact of their work on other parallel proceedings and the integrity of the system as a whole. This duty was central to UNCITRAL's transparency rules, which encourage tribunals to recognise the legitimacy of amicus curiae briefs, consider the views of third parties and hold public hearings. This remains the clear consensus of UNCITRAL States and forms the basis of current efforts to reform the ISDS system. By articulating this difference and calling on tribunals to have regard to the systemic implications of their decisions, a soft law instrument could help to facilitate coordination between proceedings and promote consistency in investment arbitration.

When considering the form such a soft law instrument might take, one might look for inspiration to the International Bar Association ("IBA"), whose soft law instruments have been regularly and successfully applied in a number of areas in the daily practice of international arbitration. These include the IBA guidelines on conflicts of interest, on party representation, and on the taking of evidence. While such guidelines are not binding, they are often treated as persuasive and authoritative by tribunals and parties due to their reflection of consensus. However, considering the current work taking place in UNCITRAL and the disconnect between practitioners (who would drive any reform effort in fora such as the IBA) and the States that created the ISDS system, a more appropriate format would be a UNGA declaration similar to those made with respect to the interpretation of Article II and VII of the New York Convention in 2006. Such a recommendation would carry significant weight and be difficult to ignore even by the most commercial arbitration minded tribunals.

In terms of content, the recommendation could include three elements. First, a formal acknowledgement of the systemic difference between investment arbitration and commercial arbitration, recognising the unique nature of investment arbitration and empowering tribunals to consider the systemic implications of their decisions without fear of overstepping their role. This is particularly important in the area of parallel proceedings, where so much depends on taking into account what may transpire outside the specific proceedings before the arbitral tribunal. Second, the recommendation could recognise a specific duty for investment tribunals to make their best efforts to coordinate related arbitrations, whether at the request of a party or of their own accord. This recognition would provide a basis for parties and their counsel to apply for coordination of proceedings with other arbitrations. Third, the recommendation could include a procedural "toolbox" with specific actions that parties and tribunals can take to fulfil the duty of best efforts.

These actions could include, first, sharing information about related proceedings, either through the Mauritius transparency regime or on a tribunal-to-tribunal basis. This would range from information such as the status of the arbitration, the procedural calendar, and so on, to full exchange of relevant evidence and submissions (for instance, to avoid inconsistent cases being made by the same or related parties). A second action might be to include the informal coordination of proceedings in terms of briefings, production of evidence, hearings, and so on. Third, tribunals could conduct concurrent hearings, which could be particularly helpful in cases where there are waves of claims against States over the same measures and facts. A fourth measure might be the aggregation of claims. The goal here would be to avoid parallel proceedings from the outset by providing guidance on when claims can be aggregated into a single case. For instance, when the claims arise from the same BIT and are based on the same State measure, aggregation should be possible (we saw the example of three Argentina mass claims cases in Chap. IV). Claims might also be aggregated where the claims are based on different but "compatible" BITs (in language reminiscent of that used for consolidation). Finally, tribunals may consider partial or full consolidation.

Cross-institution consolidation protocol

Moving on to the second potential option for incremental reform, the idea of a cross-institution consolidation protocol has already been discussed in the context of commercial arbitration with the SIAC proposal. Given space constraints, I will not delve into that topic again. I would simply note the following points.

First, all major institutions are currently participating in the UNCITRAL reform work and collaborating with the UNCITRAL Secretariat, providing hope that a consolidation protocol can be developed and agreed upon in the field of investment arbitration.

Second, attempting to include consolidation provisions solely within the rules of a single institution (whether it be ICSID, UNCITRAL or the PCA) would likely be ineffective in the realm of investment arbitration. This is because most BITs provide investors with various options for accessing investment arbitration. As a result, investors looking to avoid consolidation could simply select different rules for each claim they file (e.g. ICSID for one, UNCITRAL for another and the Stockholm Chamber of Commerce for a third).

Lastly, any protocol that focuses solely on institutions that handle investment arbitration may not address all issues, as there are often related commercial arbitrations that must be taken into account. Nor does the SIAC Protocol appear easy to transpose into the investment arbitration field without adaptation, making the possibility or developing a single protocol that addresses both commercial and investment arbitration unrealistic.

Abuse of process doctrine

Lastly with regards to incremental developments, the abuse of process doctrine may have a growing role in addressing the challenges in investment arbitration, for similar reasons to its role in commercial arbitration. We have already seen a notable example in *Orascom* v. *Algeria*[150], where the doctrine was utilised to address the issue of vertical claims. This doctrine may further evolve

---

[150] *Orascom* Final Award (31 May 2017), note 133.

to address issues that the classic doctrines of *res judicata* and issue estoppel cannot tackle. However, it should be noted that the use of the doctrine of abuse of process by tribunals, as seen in the *Orascom* decision, has been criticised by some for interfering with investors' rights to access ISDS. The validity of that criticism may be open to doubt given that the doctrine of abuse of rights operates precisely where a right (such as the right to access ISDS) would otherwise exist but is being abused. Nonetheless, it is important to acknowledge that this development remains controversial.

2. *Systemic reform*

The premise for the proponents of such reform is that the reason why the current system is so fragmented is no random occurrence, but arises out of its very nature which necessarily gives rise to a patchwork of independent tribunals created ad hoc to resolve each dispute as it arises. As a result, no amount of incremental changes can bring to this system the degree of coherence and consistency which any legitimate system of dispute resolution requires. Put differently, the problems that arise are systemic and require a systemic change.

As to the form which this systemic reform should take, the main solution which is being canvassed at UNCITRAL is that of a multilateral court with a built-in appeal mechanism which would finally resolve and settle conflicts of authorities. Such a court would in particular have the power to consolidate its proceedings and join parties, as any court does, and produce judgments with res judicata effect (at appellate level if required), which will have an impact not only on directly related claims (e.g. vertical claims) but potentially on other claims arising from the same measure or from similar facts. There is significant political support for such a solution from developing States and from the EU, and significant opposition to it from other States, and it is premature to try and fathom what exact shape it will end up taking.

Much of the resistance to the possible creation of such a permanent court system has been on the basis that – while it may theoretically resolve or alleviate many issues in this field, including that of parallel proceedings – it is bound to result in a system which will lack neutrality because it is being created by States and will thus favour States. That is not a premise which can be accepted at face value: the current ISDS system (which the same critics argue for) was itself created by States. Further, where the case for systemic reform is otherwise clear, it cannot be assumed that means cannot be found to ensure that the new court system is devised in a way which will deliver the benefits of a coherent system while preserving neutrality.

UNCITRAL is currently tasked with finding a way to establish a new court system that delivers the benefits of a coherent system while preserving neutrality. This task may hold the answer to many of the questions raised throughout this lecture.

ABOUT THE AUTHOR

BIOGRAPHICAL NOTE

Salim Abdool Hamid Moollan KC, born 26 July 1971, in Moka (Mauritius), Mauritian, French and British nationalities.

Lycée Labourdonnais, Mauritius (1981-1988), French Baccalauréat, Mathematics and Physics, mention Très Bien avec les Félicitations du Jury, Lycée Louis-le-Grand, Paris (1988-1990), classes préparatoires aux Grandes Écoles scientifiques, Ecole Polytechnique, Paris (1990-1993), Diplôme de l'Ecole Polytechnique, Advanced Mathematics and Physics, Institut d'Etudes Politiques de Paris (Sciences-Po) (1993-1995), Political Science and Economics degree, Downing College, Cambridge (1995-1997), BA (Law), First Class Honours in Part I and Part II (MA: 2001), Harris Scholarship, Senior Harris Scholarship, Inns of Court School of Law, London (1997-1998), Bar Vocational Course, Middle Temple's Queen Mother Scholarship.

Called to the Bars of England and Wales and Mauritius (1998), Queen's Counsel (2016), King's Counsel (2022).

Representative of Mauritius at the United Nations Commission on International Trade Law ("UNCITRAL") since 2006; past Chairman and Vice-Chairman of UNCITRAL and past chairman of its Working Group II (Arbitration); Vice-President of the International Court of Arbitration of the International Chamber of Commerce ("ICC") (2009-2015); Past member of the Court of the London Court of International Arbitration ("LCIA"); Visiting Professor (International Arbitration Law), King's College, University of London; Member of the World Bank's International Centre for Settlement of Investment Disputes ("ICSID") Panels of arbitrators and conciliators; Member of the UK's Department for Business, Innovations and Skills' *ad hoc* advisory group on international arbitration; Editor, *Arbitration International*; Membre du Comité de Lecture, *Revue de l'Arbitrage*; Past member of the Editorial Board of the *ICSID Review*.

Member of the Comité Français de l'Arbitrage, the Commercial Bar Association, the Institut pour l'Arbitrage International, the LCIA, the London Common Law and

Commercial Bar Association and the ICC UK Arbitration Committee.

PRINCIPAL PUBLICATIONS

"A Tale of Two Cities: l'affaire Dallah, Goldman Lecture 2022", *Arbitration International*, forthcoming.

"Rethinking International Arbitration Law in a New Arbitral Seat" [with Fedelma Smith], *Arbitration International*, forthcoming.

"Some Thoughts on Emmanuel Gaillard's 'Vertus de la règle matérielle'", in *Liber Amicorum Emmanuel Gaillard*, forthcoming.

Investment Arbitration: Dealing with the Sovereign Debt Crisis?, Permanent Court of Arbitration Series, forthcoming.

"Rethinking Jurisdiction, Competence – Competence and Separability", Permanent Court of Arbitration Series, June 2012.

"The New Mauritian International Arbitration Act 2008" [with Ricky H. Diwan], *Paris Journal of International Arbitration, Les Cahiers de l'Arbitrage*, Vol. 1 (2010), pp. 309-322.

"Une brève introduction à la nouvelle loi mauricienne sur l'arbitrage international", *Revue de l'Arbitrage* (2009), No. 4, pp. 933-941.

"Observations on the Court of Appeal's Judgment in *Sun Life Assurance Co. of Canada (Canada) and American Phoenix Life and Reassurance Co. (USA) and Phoenix Home Life Mutual Insurance Co. (USA)* v. *The Lincoln National Life Insurance Co (USA)*", in *International Arbitration Court Decisions*, 2nd ed., US, Juris Publishing, 2008, pp. 195-228.

"Article II and the Requirements of Form" [with T. T. Landau QC], in Gaillard and di Pietro (eds.), *Enforcement of Arbitration Agreements and International Arbitral Awards: The New York Convention 1958 in Practice*, UK, Cameron May, 2007, pp. 187-256.

"Chronique de jurisprudence étrangère, Royaume-Uni", *Revue de l'Arbitrage* (2006), No. 1, pp. 258-278.

"Note – Royaume-Uni Chambre des Lords, 30 juin 2005" [with V. V. Veeder QC], *Revue de l'Arbitrage* (2006), No. 4, pp. 1032-1038.

Author of the "Arbitration" chapter of the *All England Annual Review* (2004-2008).

**PUBLICATIONS
OF THE HAGUE ACADEMY
OF INTERNATIONAL LAW**

COLLECTED COURSES

Since 1923 the top names in international law have taught at The Hague Academy of International Law. All the volumes of the *Collected Courses* which have been published since 1923 are available, as, since the very first volume, they are reprinted regularly in their original format.

Since 2008, certain courses have been the subject of a pocketbook edition.

In addition, the total collection now exists in electronic form. All works already published have been put "on line" and can be consulted under one of the proposed subscription methods, which offer a range of tariffs and possibilities.

WORKSHOPS

The Academy publishes the discussions from the Workshops which it organizes. The latest title of the Workshops already published is as follows: *Topicality of the 1907 Hague Conference, the Second Peace Conference* (2007).

CENTRE FOR STUDIES AND RESEARCH

The scientific works of the Centre for Studies and Research in International Law and International Relations of The Hague Academy of International Law, the subjects of which are chosen by the Curatorium of the Academy, have been published, since the Centre's 1985 session, in a publication in which the Directors of Studies reported on the state of research of the Centre under their direction. This series has been discontinued and the title of the latest booklet published is as follows: *Rules and Institutions of International Humanitarian Law Put to the Test of Recent Armed Conflicts.* Nevertheless, when the work of the Centre has been of particular interest and originality, the reports of the Directors of Studies together with the articles by the researchers form the subject of a collection published in the series The Law Books of the Academy.

POCKETBOOKS OF THE ACADEMY

(By chronological order of publication)

1

Gaillard, E.: Aspects philosophiques du droit de l'arbitrage international, 2008, 252 pages.

(ISBN 978-90-04-17148-0)

2

Schrijver, N.: The Evolution of Sustainable Development in International Law: Inception, Meaning and Status, 2008, 276 pages.
(ISBN 978-90-04-17407-8)

3

Moura Vicente, D.: La propriété intellectuelle en droit international privé, 2009, 516 pages.

(ISBN 978-90-04-17907-3)

4

Decaux, E.: Les formes contemporaines de l'esclavage, 2009, 272 pages.
(ISBN 978-90-04-17908-0)

5

McLachlan, C.: Lis Pendens in International Litigation, 2009, 492 pages.

(ISBN 978-90-04-17909-7)

6

Carbone, S. M.: Conflits de lois en droit maritime, 2010, 312 pages.
(ISBN 978-90-04-18688-0)

7

Boele-Woelki, K.: Unifying and Harmonizing Substantive Law and the Role of Conflict of Laws, 2010, 288 pages.
(ISBN 978-90-04-18683-5)

8

Onuma, Y.: A Transcivilizational Perspective in International Law, 2010, 492 pages.
(ISBN 978-90-04-18689-7)

9

Bucher, A.: La dimension sociale du droit international privé. Cours général, 2011, 552 pages.
(ISBN 978-90-04-20917-6)

10

Thürer, D.: International Humanitarian Law: Theory, Practice, Context, 2011, 504 pages.   (ISBN 978-90-04-17910-3)

11

Alvarez, J. E.: The Public International Law Regime Governing International Investment, 2011, 504 pages.
(ISBN 978-90-04-18682-8)

12

Wang, G.: Radiating Impact of WTO on Its Members' Legal System: The Chinese Perspective, 2011, 384 pages.
(ISBN 978-90-04-21854-3)

13

Bogdan, M.: Private International Law as Component of the Law of the Forum, 2012, 360 pages.
(ISBN 978-90-04-22634-0)

14

Davey, W. J.: Non-discrimination in the World Trade Organization: The Rules and Exceptions, 2012, 360 pages.
(ISBN 978-90-04-23314-0)

15

Xue Hanqin: Chinese Contemporary Perspectives on International Law — History, Culture and International Law, 2012, 288 pages.
(ISBN 978-90-04-23613-4)

16

Reisman, W. M.: The Quest for World Order and Human Dignity in the Twenty-first Century: Constitutive Process and Individual Commitment. General Course on Public International Law, 2012, 504 pages.
(ISBN 978-90-04-23615-8)

17

Dugard, J.: The Secession of States and Their Recognition in the Wake of Kosovo, 2013, 312 pages.
(ISBN 978-90-04-25748-1)

18

Gannagé, L.: Les méthodes du droit international privé à l'épreuve des conflits de cultures, 2013, 372 pages.
(ISBN 978-90-04-25750-4)

19

Kohler, Ch.: L'autonomie de la volonté en droit international privé : un principe universel entre libéralisme et étatisme, 2013, 288 pages.

(ISBN 978-90-04-25752-8)

20

Kreindler, R.: Competence-Competence in the Face of Illegality in Contracts and Arbitration Agreements, 2013, 504 pages.

(ISBN 978-90-04-25754-2)

21

Crawford, J.: Chance, Order, Change: The Course of International Law. General Course on Public International Law, 2014, 540 pages.

(ISBN 978-90-04-26808-1)

22

Brand, R. A.: Transaction Planning Using Rules on Jurisdiction and the Recognition and Enforcement of Judgments, 2014, 360 pages.

(ISBN 978-90-04-26810-4)

23

Kolb, R.: L'article 103 de la Charte des Nations Unies, 2014, 416 pages.

(ISBN 978-90-04-27836-3)

24

Benvenisti, E.: The Law of Global Governance, 2014, 336 pages. (ISBN 978-90-04-27911-7)

25

Yusuf, A. A.: Pan-Africanism and International Law, 2014, 288 pages.

(ISBN 978-90-04-28504-0)

26

Kono, T.: Efficiency in Private International Law, 2014, 216 pages.

(ISBN 978-90-04-28506-4)

27

Cachard, O., Le transport international aérien de passagers, 2015, 292 pages. (ISBN 978-90-04-29773-9)

28

Corten, O.: La rébellion et le droit international, 2015,
376 pages.

(ISBN 978-90-04-29775-3)

29

Frigo, M., Circulation des biens culturels, détermination de la
loi applicable et méthodes de règlement des litiges, 2016,
552 pages.

(ISBN 978-90-04-32129-8)

30

Bermann, G. A., International Arbitration and Private International Law, 2017, 648 pages.

(ISBN 978-90-04-34825-7)

31

Bennouna, M., Le droit international entre la lettre et l'esprit,
2017, 304 pages.

(ISBN 978-90-04-34846-2)

32

Murphy, S., International Law relating to Islands, 376 pages.
(ISBN 978-90-04-36154-6)

33

Hess, B., The Private-Public Law Divide in International
Dispute Resolution, 328 pages.

(ISBN 978-90-04-38490-3)

34

Rau, A.: The Allocation of Power between Arbitral Tribunals
and State Courts, 2018, 608 pages.

(ISBN 978-90-04-38891-8)

35

Muir Watt, H.: Discours sur les méthodes du droit international
privé (des formes juridiques de l'inter-altérité, 2019, 608
pages.

(ISBN 978-90-04-39558-9)

36

Nolte, G.: Treaties and Their Practice – Symptoms of Their
Rise or Decline, 2018, 288 pages.

(ISBN 978-90-04-39456-8)

37

Cuniberti, G.: Le fondement de l'effet des jugements étrangers, 2019, 288 pages.   (ISBN 978-90-04-41180-7)

38

D'Avout, L.: L'entreprise et les conflits internationaux de lois, 875 pages.   (ISBN 978-90-04-41668-0)

39

Brown Weiss, E.: Establishing Norms in a Kaleidoscopic World, 528 pages.   (ISBN 978-90-04-42200-1)

40

Brunnée, J.: Procedure and Substance in International Environmental Law, 2020, 240 pages.
                    (ISBN 978-90-04-44437-9)

41

Rajamani, L.: Innovation and Experimentation in the International Climate Change Regime, 2020, 336 pages.
                    (ISBN 978-90-04-44439-3)

42

Kessedjian, C.: Le tiers impartial et indépendant en droit international, juge, arbitre, médiateur, conciliateur, 2020, 832 pages.   (ISBN 978-90-04-44880-3)

43

Maljean-Dubois, S.: Le droit international de la biodiversité, 2021, 590 pages.   (ISBN 978-90-04-46287-8)

44

Dasser, F.: "Soft Law" in International Commercial Arbitration, 2021, 300 pages.   (ISBN 978-90-04-46289-2)

45

Peters, A.: Animals in International Law, 2021, 641 pages.
                    (ISBN 978-90-04-46624-1)

46

Besson, S.: La *due diligence* en droit international, 2021, 363 pages.   (ISBN 978-90-04-46626-5)

47

Ferrari, F.: Forum Shopping Despite Unification of Law, 2021, 446 pages.   (ISBN 978-90-04-50291-8)

48

Wolfrum, R.: Solidarity and Community Interests: Driving Forces for the Interpretation and Development of International Law, 2021, 663 pages.

(ISBN 978-90-04-50832-3)

49

Kolb, R.: Le droit international comme corps de « droit privé » et de « droit public », 2022, 967 pages.

(ISBN 978-90-04-51836-0)

50

Tladi, D.: The Extraterritorial Use of Force against Non-State Actors, 2022, 193 pages.   (ISBN 978-90-04-52147-6)

51

Schabas, W. A.: Relationships between International Criminal Law and Other Branches of International Law, 2022, 272 pages.   (ISBN 978-90-04-52149-0)

52

Bollée, S.: Les pouvoirs inhérents des arbitres internationaux, 2023, 306 pages.   (ISBN 978-90-04-67848-4)

53

Laghmani, S.: Islam et droit international, 2023, 168 pages.

(ISBN 978-90-04-67850-7)

54

Kovács, P.: L'indidividu et sa position devant la Cour pénale internationale, 528 pages.

(ISBN 978-90-04-69428-6)

[A paraître en 2024]

Stephan, P. B.: Applying Municipal Law in International Disputes.
Blokker, N.: Legal Facets of the Practice of International Organizations.
Corten, O.: Le champ juridique international.
Lim, C. L.: The Aims and Methods of Postcolonial International Law.

Printed in February 2024
by Triangle Bleu,
59600 Maubeuge (France)

Setting: R. Mirland,
59870 Warlaing (France)

55/02-24.